Your Father
on the Train of Ghosts

Your Father
on the Train of Ghosts

Poems by
G.C. Waldrep
and John Gallaher

AMERICAN POETS CONTINUUM SERIES, No. 126

BOA Editions, Ltd. ❧ Rochester, NY ❧ 2011

First Edition
11 12 13 14   7 6 5 4 3 2 1

For information about permission to reuse any material from this book please contact The
Permissions Company at www.permissionscompany.com or e-mail permdude@eclipse.net.

Publications by BOA Editions, Ltd.—a not-for-profit corporation under section 501 (c) (3)
of the United States Internal Revenue Code—are made possible with funds from a variety of
sources, including public funds from the New York State Council on the Arts, a state agency;
the Literature Program of the National Endowment for the Arts; the County of Monroe, NY;
the Lannan Foundation for support of the Lannan Translations Selection Series; the Sonia
Raiziss Giop Charitable Foundation; the Mary S. Mulligan Charitable Trust; the Roches-
ter Area Community Foundation; the Arts & Cultural Council for Greater Rochester; the
Steeple-Jack Fund; the Ames-Amzalak Memorial Trust in memory of Henry Ames, Semon
Amzalak and Dan Amzalak; and contributions from many individuals nationwide.

See Colophon on page 230 for special individual acknowledgments.

Cover Art and Design: Sandy Knight
Interior Design and Composition: Richard Foerster
Manufacturing: McNaughton & Gunn
BOA Logo: Mirko

Library of Congress Cataloging-in-Publication Data

Waldrep, G.C., 1968–
Your father on the train of ghosts / by G.C. Waldrep and John Gallaher. —1st ed.
   p. cm.
ISBN 978-1-934414-48-4
I. Gallaher, John, 1965– II. Title.
PS3623.A358Y68 2011
811.6—dc22
                                    2010029675

BOA Editions, Ltd.
250 North Goodman Street, Suite 306
Rochester, NY 14607
www.boaeditions.org
A. Poulin, Jr., Founder (1938–1996)

NATIONAL
ENDOWMENT
FOR THE ARTS
A great nation
deserves great art.

State of the Arts

NYSCA

CONTENTS

II

Like somebody knocking on your door at three in the morning, you know. And you try to pretend that you aren't breathing.

—Jack Spicer

Did we live in a constellation? Did it explode?

—Carla Harryman

I

AUTOMATED TOWN

The automated town is purchasing
a compass of afternoons. Look, I'm bored
and empty too. What do you want? This room is nothing
but racks of clothes. See how easy it is? That one,
sides of beef. This one is people
for the hanging. That one is religions. See, you
didn't call. I thought you were going to call. That one
is rows of vegetables. This one is popular music. That room
is racks of car parts. And you (not your real name)
go out and back. You needed something
or something to do. It's your automated corner
in the automated town. That one is sex toys
and lubricants. Because it always comes out
happy. Because it was the first idea
that came to me. Or these are the people in my
neighborhood. One works on cars. One works
at the town transfer station. One runs a distributorship.
One builds cabinets. One used to be
a sheriff, until he had to quit. It was
a movie once. The whole town killed someone. The clock
read 10:10 and we realized we were in an advertisement.
I could drive there. It's about two hours
away. I could have lunch there and ask the waitress.
She could show me the rooms. And this one
is rows of foreign students. That one
is musical instruments. It's about finding the next thing.
It's a room of hibachis. You got off work
and you went home. It was almost midnight. It was
mid-afternoon. You should ride a bicycle more. You
should drink more water and less
of everything else. It's a room of people dressed
in bright clothes. It's a room of hanging doors.
Of cell phones and one is ringing. Of people having sex.

Rows of bottles of vodka. Rows of
sparklers. We could go on like this for some time,
so we do. Bugs are flying in and out of the open
windows. All the TVs are on.

THE BABY CATALOGUES

When the city gets in the way
unexpectedly, all the actuaries and accountants
start consulting the baby catalogues.

Each is looking for his baby, or hers.

All the babies in the baby catalogues
are dressed in the same gray uniforms.
This, say the authorities,

is to prevent sentimental misidentification.

Across the city, deep in their offices,
the actuaries and accountants
wish they could remember
just where or how they lost their babies.

They wish they could remember
whether the babies they lost were boys
or girls, what they were wearing

or where they were at the time,
at the theater, or strolling through
one of the larger municipal parks.

In the photographs, the babies look
content, vaguely knowing.

Outside, the city is experimenting
with its new wardrobe,
primping and preening before the enormous
mirror the ocean makes.
It is difficult to see past the city

when the city gets like this,

no longer trying to sell you anything,
no longer thinking of you at all.

THE HOUSE RHAPSODY

For the difficulty of dinner tables,
or to figure out how things work, the family
is sitting in a circle on the floor.

They bend, as bodies bend,
into the catalogue of the room,
or the room floating up around them.

The family is standing
in various entrances. The family is sitting.
"I wasn't thinking of anything

specific," they say, each facing the room
from one of the various
entrances. The difficulty,

and what do we have to say about it,
and what do we have to show for it
around the dinner table,

or the sound like a dinner table. Each with a place
and no memory. "Let us rise
to the invitation of the room," they say.

They say, "Can you relax this once,
from the cheap seats." The lights
and the distance through evening.

It's there in everybody, somewhere,
the family says. The table of wood
and the room in orange.

The silverware floating past. The caught glimpses
of napkins. And look how calm we are.
Look at our beauty.

YOUR NEW BIRTHDAY

You sink when you think about it. You sink
when you think about
other things, up again at night, the town slowing, shifting
back and forth.

The dolls are around the doll table
having a pretend doll party.

It's four in the morning. They're in the window
of the only room with the lights on
in the house.

A figure in the dark around the garage,

and the different things animals can do
which make them look almost like people
for a second, until you blink.

Which is make-believe.

In the child museum it's 4 a.m.

You wake, and all the squirrels of the city are in a circle
around your bed, watching you intently.

FROM WHICH MORTAR CITIES RISE

The movie is about sand,
about the cool indifference that lies
at the heart of sand.

We lie on the sand
and watch the movie about sand

with our 3-D glasses on.

The movie goes on and on;
somehow we never get tired,
or sleepy, or bored,

or even sunburned, though
the sun is bright. It comes up,
then it goes down,

and then it comes up again.
Sometimes we adjust our glasses,
or drink from a plastic jug.

At night, we expect
to see the moon—
the real moon, I mean, not

the moon in the film,
which is buried beneath the sand,

which is the sand's cool heart.

Night without the moon
is hardly night at all.
It's like a desert that has mistaken

itself for a plague.
It's like an army
that has lost its library card.

The 3-D glasses
make everything look more real,
but not more interesting,
not necessarily.

And so we turn our attentions
back to the movie.

THE ANODYNES

All the fathers of Indiana
are falling from a window. All the fathers
of Indiana, for reasons unknown,
are falling.

The windows are bright and white,
like bridges. The fathers of Indiana
are so modern
they haven't happened yet.

All mystery is defective,
they say.

It's a breezy day. Wind through the windows.
The headaches return. They cross the bridges
into the city.
They exit the tunnels into the city.

This much is for certain. It's a box
of wires and gears,
and we call it a city. We name the bridges
after our children. We follow
our children across the bridges.

They do everything twice here,
while the lucky things whisper everything
is OK. In that,
they're like the unlucky things.

There's a train going by. There it goes,
right through your hands.

THE ARCHAEOLOGISTS

There was singing in the tunnel
for as long as the food held out. After that,
we dug more feverishly:
no more jokes about mothers-in-law,
no more looking backward.

Sometimes, we chanced upon the ruins
of some previous civilization:

tumbled blocks, limestone, marble, basalt;
temples and parliaments.

Other times, even in the squalid light,
we could tell we were working
through more modest habitations:

a child's doll, a burst wireless,
a few flaking pots and pans.

Philip said he knew
when we were digging through a house
where a beautiful woman had once
lived. He said he could taste it:
the earth tasted different, in those places.

We checked our manuals, our histories.
The soil had grown softer;
some of us thought
we were digging through graves.

Still, Philip said—don't you remember?

The way her cheeks glistened
with oil, in the plaza, on summer evenings?
The magazines in her bathroom?

That thing she used to do,
when she was feeling good, with her hair?

ANNIVERSARIES OF BAD THINGS

The pan flashes, and soon the whole house
is burning down. Circles of light around the yard,
as if it could be some other way than what it is
where we're between what's happening
and some alternate meanwhile
where the tulips droop in the vase all afternoon
getting more and more gray.

And what happens next is anybody's big guess,
like having to stand in line at some counter
and taking a number, only to find it's the wrong counter,
the wrong building, the wrong part in some life
you stumbled into, ill-prepared.

The children sigh, then it's off to California
and one of those diseases you have to keep convincing people
is real. "Listen," they say, or, "Look,"
either way it's directed at you
as if you've just knocked a vase over
or stepped in a vase someone spilled, the like of which
will never be seen again, they claim.

First, your phone is ringing, then
you're the tree by the highway
where someone's just buried you.
They're calling your name all over the place
where the light is better, and you feel
you could almost touch them, they're so close.

Maybe such things are only helpful
in the telling, we think, so we hold hands
and form a chain, calling ourselves the tide
or rolling with the tide, watching the toy shovels

that line the field. "Start whispering," the woman beside you whispers. "It's all we have."

ADVICE TO PASSENGERS

There is a man, there is a woman,
and there is a child.

Their faces too plain,
their mouths too wide.

It's a grim business. You can feel it piling up
however quiet you refuse to be.

Watch them.

They woke up one morning
and their hands were all rubber.

"How can you hold me?"
they asked.
"How can I feel you?"

They woke up
and their voices were coming through
on the radio,
saying, "I should've warned you."

It would seem easy enough
to warn someone.

They are at the window
in the sunlight.

Step back a bit.

Don't forget to thank them
for their time.

ELEGY FOR THE MANHATTAN PROJECT

In the catalogue of mistakes
there is this page you've dog-eared.
It has to do with hope
and with the nature of friendship.
It's next to the page ticking off the many
disappointments of broadcast news.

Every few weeks you pick up the volume,
thumb your way to the page.

On television, beautiful men and women
are debating your latest faux pas:
The way you insulted
the very person you were trying
to apologize to, accidentally
but also maybe just a little on purpose;

the way you depleted the oil supply.
The way you bombed Iraq.

You look across the page
and feel comforted, a bit, knowing
newscasters have their own
instruction manuals, their own rituals
of contrition and repentance.

Then the buzzer rings: someone's
at the door, a man carrying
a bouquet, maybe, or with some food
you must have ordered,

the woman falling in flames
from the fire escape. The enormous cake
with the sharp knife hidden inside.

TRADE DEFICIT

Do you have any
friends, the darkness asks,
and for a moment
you're surprised: you expected
salt, maybe, or *terror.*

China has some wisdom
to offer on this point:
Learn how to make
a lot of things that are basically
useless and also
a few things that matter, then
flood the markets.

The trick is that once
the markets are flooded,
you must create new markets.

Darkness does this
all the time, knocking
at your door: *Do you have any*
mercy, it asks, *any weapons,*
any sugar, any stone.

YOUR LOVER, LATER

Your lover is on the roof.
The gray roof. Your lover is sitting on the roof
of that house you remember. Your lover long ago
sitting there
with both hands down. Your lover
sitting there waving
into the pockets of air.

It's an easy idea.

All the people of the town are out
on their roofs. Little people
over their porch lights. Legs over the edges
like many high
and beautiful things.

And one of them is your lover. Remember?
Some of them you can see, and some not.
Call to them. Why not call to them

and then listen all night.
All night the sound of that town.
Your lover on the roof
and a train along the horizon
that's crowded with hotels.

The Ford dealership is setting off
balloons, red and blue and green and
white balloons.

I'd like to climb up there. It would be
such an easy concept. Such an easy way to be.

And what about your lover? It's such a large town,
isn't it? So many roofs
and so many people
with their hands at their sides
in the future. It's easy. It must be.

Tell me again what to do.

ELEMENTAL PICTURE OF BOATS IN THE DISTANCE

We were facing the boats and the boats
were sailing.

The panic of boats in the lake all summer.

The panic of children on the shore,
watching the panic of the boats.

They're calling to each other
and raising their hands under a bright sky
and through the trees to the water
all afternoon.

They had tables set up,
and pavilions.

They had drinks and grass and hotdogs.

I heard it all day
the way I heard it.

The sun on the metal of the playground,
and the hot sun
on the picnic tables.

ELEGY FOR THE MOST PEOPLE

A train promises
that it will never leave you
alone,.in somebody else's apartment,
with a sick cat to take care of,

and you believe it. You believe the train
because you think, deep down,

that the train wants to take you
somewhere else,

which is a confusion
of desire and location, trust
and vector, but that's OK, because

now another train is promising
that it will never
come to you in the middle of the night

as a cold and steady rain,
and you believe this too,
because it seems so unlikely

that a hollow sheath of chromium and steel
could somehow transform itself
into weather.
You think this is the train

you would like to take, maybe,
when suddenly

another train steps in, and promises
that it will be a sort of music
for you,

and another promises
it will be like a contact lens
over the eye of your soul, and yet another
assures you in all sincerity

it will become a pollen
that will never make you sneeze,
and from which
zinnias will grow.

And you believe these trains, all of them,
in the same way you believe
in ghosts, with their daguerreotypes
and ramekins of salt,

that keep coming and going, presumably
wanting you to do
something *for* them, or maybe go

with them, though believing *in* them
doesn't really change anything:

the half-light in the plaza,
the broken clock on the mantelpiece,
the conference invitation;

the new etymologies of silence
and the machineries we keep inventing
to record them, to tell us

just what it is we're not hearing, to keep
us where we already are.

SPACE TO THE WEST

When the space is disrupted by presence, we can always stop
    for tea.

Because the sun rises and then the sun sets.

Then, many things become probable: sanitary conditions,
    the broken yellow lines and broken white lines, and the
    gorgeous new you.

And because it is America both times.

The space encounters one from various protuberances,
    causing the road to rise and communication to fade and
    to return.

Upon returning, we thought the place hadn't changed much.

Because I had wanted to say "doth rise," but didn't.

You want to lose a few pounds and you'd love to look
    younger as well, but to keep accruing experiences.

One can make a list of one's spaces and place it on a postcard
    with a picture of a rabbit with horns.

For the first time, one can make new demarcations of time
    so that "for the first time" may happen at any time one
    wishes.

Because the disbeliever and the unbeliever agree on some
    things and disagree on others.

You'll feel better after a good night's sleep.

"Picasso is Painting," read the sign, though Picasso has been
    dead many years.

In other times, what if that mountain over there were more or
    less the feeling of events upon that mountain?

What a bird might change, later, kept us busy for a time at
    the roadside diner, looking off to the red hills.

Later, when the hills turn to face the light, the hills
    are material, and flare the way we noticed the space
    becoming.

The space describes itself in the manner we find most
    pleasing.

We touch the window, and the world floats.

OUTSIDE THE ELEVATOR MUSEUM

The first thing we do
is set fire to the tents. It's possible
there are people, or things, or maybe animals
inside the tents
when we set fire to them,
but that's not really part of our problem.

The revolution moves on
in several directions at once. That's
how we know
it's the revolution, say the scientists.

If we back away far enough
from the museum, we can see the shadow
puppetry the city is busy untying
from the market economy.
There is fighting in the streets,
but no more than usual for this time of year.

Oddly enough, the elevator museum
is only one storey. We think
maybe it goes down a ways, into the earth.

Eventually, new patrons
will bring new tents from the armory,
new animals, new theories
about what comes next and how to get there.

Particles of the revolution
keep spinning off into the outer recesses
of what we call space. That's how we know
it's the revolution, say the scientists,
standing like the rest of us
outside the museum, waiting for it to open.

A SHORT HISTORY OF FRIENDSHIP

We were all together in this nightclub
where fire was performing: here
fire forms a hoop and then jumps through itself,
here fire is shot from a cannon, here
fire saws fire in half. The music was loud
and the laser show played over the soybean fields
and parked cars, so that what looked like
part of the performance
was often just a lightning bug, or a planet,
a chip of mica in the road. We clapped anyway.
Drinks were on the house.
When we climbed to the roof, we thought
we might spend a few hours
you know, talking, getting to know each other
better. But then suddenly
there wasn't a roof anymore,
and you asked what it was
we were standing on, and I looked down,
the way you do in a cartoon or against your will
when somebody says "Look"
and you realize it was only
a pop-top, or a shadow, a glob of flattened gum
or maybe just somebody's idea of a joke.
That was when fire decided
to come back on stage for an encore—
a complicated act
involving knives and tigers,
a map of Portugal, a symphony by Bizet
and us, apparently, as a reporter and a policeman
trying to interview the same subject
which was fire, of course,
playing each of us off against the other
until the real reporters and policeman arrived

taking names and statements,
handing out little bits
of the Swiss chocolate you'd said we might try
some other time, in some other town,
when you weren't so full from dinner
and the smoke wasn't quite as thick
and you had something to wipe your hands on.

IN THE FILE OF DISCONTINUED THINGS

It looks like no one's showing up
again. But let's do the show anyway. The one called
Lincoln. Or *Ban the Bomb*.

There's a reason for it
as there are reasons for most things. Smoke.
Chocolate. The way old paint
looks like a sunburn. The floor
of overlapping shadows
from the television
and approaching fires.

Let's say the show is over, or everything
is over. The next show or the war show,
where the teenage male is obsessing
over girls, which we take to mean teenage males
obsess over girls. It's late,

I'm watching television
while reading the Constitution. Which is easy. (We
the floor shine.) (In order to
order faster delivery.)

It's winter. And snow. Whole wedding gowns
of snow. Towns under wraps
and we know this already. Hey,

let's be the town anyway. We are free
for a limited time.

We can go to the show where no one goes.

GUN CONTROL IN THE OCCUPATION

In the first field, you feel the wind
blowing lightly against your shoulders.
Since this is the first wind
you've felt, you label it wind number one.
It's a wide field, and pleasant,

and you enjoy the play of current
against your cheeks,
round your bare arms.
Really, it's more of a breeze.

Eventually, you come to a second field
where the air is a little
more insistent, though the temperature
remains warm. It's not exactly

as if it were blowing
out of some desert, rather
as if it—the wind—
were remembering what it was like
to blow out of some desert.
You blink a little against the grit
it churns from the sillions.

Before you know it
you find yourself
in a third field, fallow this year,
and you register what you think of
as your third wind,

chilly—the steady, determined sort
that blows in late fall and early spring.

You pull a windbreaker on.
You can see last year's furrows
beneath your feet.
The grasshoppers spring away from you
and the weeds are already beginning
to go brown and stringy.

And then, without much warning,
you know you must be
in a fourth field, because this wind
is new, a winter wind,
harsh, malevolent, a wind

that has imagined murder.
And you wish you could turn back
to the first field, where the breeze
was so pleasant,

or maybe further yet,
but you find you no longer recall

what came before:
whether it was good land or sorry,
whether you enjoyed it,
whether there was any wind at all.

CARS MOVING AT REASONABLE SPEEDS

We kept looking for the parkway
in the vicinity of the park,
but all we kept finding
was each other, I mean more of us,

those who had come here
looking for
something else, or someone else.

It was the same
in the botanical gardens,
at the glider rental stations,
around the food courts,

by the riprap of the wading pools.

There were some thickets
we didn't bother to explore

and some dogs
that barked at us from a distance.
We couldn't see the dogs

but we knew they were there.

We made soothing,
consoling sounds
when we came upon their owners

on the gravel paths,
leashes held limply, almost
gently in their pale hands:

It was the sort of loss
we could relate to, or rather,
a certain familiar

idea about loss. Don't blame yourself,
we told everybody we ran into.
It could happen to anyone.

DOMESTIC LIGHT

You bought the lamp at the lamp store
and then the lamp shade at the lamp shade store,
which, even at the time,
seemed like an absurd thing, a lamp shade store.
But it was an exciting place, really,

with all sorts of interesting lamp accoutrements,
things you'd never guessed anybody
could match up with a lamp, make work

with a lamp. One shade purported
to take the light of a normal 60-watt bulb
and make it seem as if
your living room were a seventeenth-century
Japanese butterfly garden. It never occurred to you
that this might be something someone might ask
of a living room, or a 60-watt bulb,

or of light itself. You suppose
this must be part of the genius of marketing.
You didn't buy that lamp shade, or the one
claiming to replicate the exact light

in the kitchens of Versailles,
or the one simulating the sun setting perfectly
over the Indian Ocean at Perth,

or even that strange one you found in the back,
a little shopworn, half-off, that promised
the particular Mediterranean light
of railyards on the edge of Athens,
circa 1920. What you wanted was more light
to read a book by: not just any book

but a certain book, one you'd been saving.
A book about birds, and about what you believe

about people, other people I mean,

the way they stand around on beaches
sometimes, in ones and twos

at dawn, the way they invented punctuation,

the way they so rarely mean what they say
and what to do about it,
and how to behave at parties,
and how the last time you saw your father

he was waving back at you, the sun glinting
off his hair, your hair, off the broken toys
someone had left scattered

in the neighbor's enormous front yard.

THE CITY EXPERIMENT

We spent all night on the city experiment,
but the thing barely moved, and now
we're worried. The formula looked good
in the congratulatory lighting, and we had this feeling
we might be able to push through to the other side
and it would turn out to be a movie set,
and you'd be walking the carpet
to an award show. Yes, you immersed yourself
in that role. Yes, you believed you were indeed that person
up there, and thank you, it sure was something,
and of course you're going to miss it
now and then, but next season it'll be a museum
or some people digging in a field.

There were other things we liked, of course,
when it wasn't important to be careful,
and the weather cooperated, with the knowledge
that this moment's going to be repeatable
and more comfortable than the boats
we used to like, but still with the feeling
that maybe it really isn't all that repeatable
after all, or at least not with you. But at that moment
the cocktails arrived, so we crested,
and whatever we said fit, or fit well enough. Yes
to the cocktail, because we're polite.

And wasn't it warm in the sun
through this window in winter,
the snow outside? I'm sure it's something small
we've overlooked. What type of cocktail,
perhaps. Perhaps survival is a state of mind,
in your floating future, there in the city experiment,
past the tennis courts and trees, and an old harmonium

someone put out by the curb, a trace
of broken china, a fleeting study of a figure
in a landscape, until you're writing notes on a napkin
that blows into the lake, and you're hearing the flat echo,
some harbor gone dark into ordinary things.

YOUR FATHER ON THE TRAIN OF GHOSTS

Your father steps on board the train of ghosts.
You watch him from the platform:

somehow, he doesn't look as old
as you expected him to be.

You think this must have something to do
with the light, or maybe

how much bigger the train is.
It stretches down the track
a long way, as far as your eyes can make out.

It's like a black bullet
that keeps speeding toward you,
you think, and then:

No, it's like a very long train, that's all.

Somewhere on board the train, your father
is choosing a seat. Maybe

he's already found one, has settled in,

picked up a magazine or newspaper
someone else left lying there,

is flipping through it, idly.
Maybe he's looking out the window, for you
you would like to think, waving,

only you'll never see it
because of the reflected glare.

Or maybe he's not looking for you at all.
Maybe he's watching the hot-air balloons
that have just appeared

all over the sky, ribbed like airborne hearts
of the giants Jack killed.

In the stories, Jack has no father.
This would explain a lot, you are thinking

as the train begins to pull away:

his misplaced affections,
stealing the harp of gold that played
all by itself. Around you,

men and women and children
are standing on the platform, shouting, waving,
hugging themselves.
The wind is cold; it must be March.

You would want that kind of music
if you were Jack, wouldn't you?

DAILY LIFE IN CLASSICAL ANTIQUITY

No one remembers what it was for,
which seems troublesome, but only
if we think about it. If at some point
one of us decided, "let's do this," and we've been doing it
ever since, or if one of us, out on a deck
overlooking a lake, said, "let's do it this other way now,"
then what's been slowly sneaking around the houses
and looking in the odd window,
is this other way not to remember,
how the first thing would be to blue the mullions
and put some greenery around the place,
then to hide some people and music
in something that looks like a rock, or a rock
on top of a rock. At some point
you might be able to whisper to everyone at once,
or to try out one of your bits, because you're cute
and the universe is unknowable.

They're over by the pool now, not wondering anything special
outside of conversational probabilities
and basic human nature. We do what we can,
passing the telephone around the circle
and wishing up plenty of birds and bright shirts,
under which some basic conception of things
might mingle with the things themselves,
giving us a little more to hope for
than how fragile our legs look, and don't the clouds look soft
as well. They're motioning to you,
saying isn't that a bright star, or an airplane
on some sleepy pursuit of another city
nearly as remarkable as all the other unrecorded journeys
we've been meaning to get around to
and watch from the other side, sooner or later,

standing with the emergency personnel,
pointing in several directions at once.

THE CIRCUS OF PROBABLE SIGHS

We're at the circus, and we're waiting—
all of us—in the risers, but nobody's come out yet.

There's no music
and the klieg lights are misty, unfocused.
When you got up a little while ago

to try to find some popcorn, cotton candy maybe,
the concession stands were empty.
There's this great hush under the bigtop:

No tigers. No clowns. No acrobats
flinging their bodies across the deckled firmament.
Somebody should demand their money back,
you think. *But that would be*

rude, the woman sitting next to you
thinks back, *and besides, consider the children.*

You consider the children.
Some of them are starting to whine now;
others have gone to sleep in their seats.

Maybe this is good for them,
you think. Maybe they should get used to life's
disappointments,
like when you think you've walked

into a marriage, or a convenience store,
only to find it was always

something else, a dry-cleaning establishment
or a Pentecostal chapel,
something that wasn't about you at all.

"I think," you start to say to the woman,
but she shushes you, holds a hand
cupped to one ear. You listen,
but all you can hear is your own breathing
and the wind against the canvas outside.

Then, in the half-light of the center ring,
something moves. You crane your neck
forward, wanting to see,

but it's only a stray dog
that has somehow found its way inside the tent.
It looks tired, a little mangy, maybe.
It probably has fleas.
It climbs the tiers of seats, wagging its tail.

Some people reach out to pet it;
others don't. *Isn't that just like
people*, the woman sitting next to you thinks

as the dog moves closer.
You wonder whether this isn't really part of the act.
You wonder what you will do
when the dog gets to you, and whether

you're not part of the act too,
come to think of it—

If you were, would that change anything?
Would anything be more interesting, or better?

ALL TRAINS LEAVING PENN STATION
ARE GHOST TRAINS

It would be good to be riding a train
and go wherever the train takes you.

The train surrounded by trains
and distant, sunny fields. The train
with a sufficiency of stoppages. Later,
the train can rattle out stories
of those who go
and those who stay.

"I'll be leaving now," you say. And
you love people like that. I saw you once on a train
when you were in love that way. I saw you
through the windows between trains.

The trains are passing notes.

It would be good to step out on the platform.
It would be good to rise
over the scab edges of the city.

The train circled the train all night
waiting for the children to come downstairs. Waiting
for the city to begin.

What notes surround these notes? And whose train,
where the people talked so much
all day and all night? The trains are hollow,
and even then it would be good.

It would be good, I promise.

THE BRIDGE AT REST

The bridge is dreaming again.

In favor of the present moment,
the bridge is dreaming
or we're dreaming of a bridge.

Cables in great arcs.

This is where I sit
with the convergence. How full
the everything else, where the traffic moves through
certain days,

rows above rows
and circling sky.

The bridge is dreaming of people
in great arcs.

I read it in the newspapers.

One calls it "leaping"
and one calls it "jumping." One calls it "to pour,"
and one calls it "to fill."

And it's two worlds.
The direction called Getting There,
where they waited and waited.

So that now
your body is most things

over the city,
in favor of the present moment.

And what are we going to say then?

ERROR AS BEAUTY

Because what is expected is only as beautiful
as expectation allows. Because it only works
as possibility, a trace of innocence
that can only come near futility, and futility
is the only explanation, the error of all things done
or not done, things that are coming to their moment,
the ship in flames, the final flames nearing
where all trace of the future is written
as something other, something unplanned
but continually unfolding, the carnage of the face
slowly turning into a child's face. The beauty of the face
rising into its own impossible moment,
the holding no one holds, the realization
there is nothing more to do, the almost question
that is the end, the calendar uncoiling
in a moment past the moment. We stand at the leading
edge of the continent. We pay good money.
We help roll out the carpet. We bring our photographs,
our songs. The fight and the show. Because we are expected
and plain, the sum of our flaws that we fall into
is one hesitation, one crumbling knowledge
of things standing and falling before us
and after. That hover. The scroll telling who and what
by seconds. The city becomes the shadow of the city.
What did we say then. Who were our desires.
Because you can stand or sit or lie down. The plan
of the movement, the moment. We could make
a killing. We could ride this out. Because
we are going long before we're gone.
And this wind every year. This picture. There's
no moment to decide. There's no
plan. No song. There's no retreat. For beauty.
I can't go any farther, as there is no farther

to go. There's no going. Because if you're going to go, you have to go for nothing. And nothing rises.

UNIVERSITY PARK

It's late at night, and we're at home together
with nothing but the cat to keep us company.
I know what you're thinking. You're thinking,
What if all the hominids all came home tonight,

at the same time, and you couldn't tell them
apart? Gorillas and chimps, mandrills and orangs
and who knows what all. What would you do?
This is what you are thinking as outside

the rain pounds on the synthetic, scaling
shingles of our roof, on the roof of the house
next to ours and on the roof of the house next to it
and a hundred other roofs on a hundred other

houses: all except for the house that has
no roof. This is the house where the people live
who know what they would do if all the apes
arrived tonight in one brougham, one package

deal. You think this is the house you would want
to live in, if you had a choice. I'm telling you:
you have a choice. You can let all our stuff
get wet, or you can keep it dry. You can know

the name of every ape, or else you could just
wave them all in, distribute typewriters
and fountain pens, dial out for pizza, not worry
so much about everything. These are *apes,*

after all: they know how to survive in the wild,
are familiar with tools, can even acquire

a certain amount of ASL. The people
who live in that other house would let them in.

The people who live in that other house
wouldn't sweat the names. When the apes come,
it's really not about you at all. They want
dinner, maybe to get a little writing done. Maybe

they want to get out of the rain, or maybe
they're enjoying the rain. Invite them in
anyway. That's what I think *I* would do. I mean,
if you're asking. If you really want to know.

MEDITATION ON SUBJECTS

So it seems the body is this tent
you stand behind. You walk around a bit
and the body's just standing there. You come back
to renegotiate, and the tent's moved
to the front yard, hovering somewhere
between big and large.

The neighbors will see, right? They're sure
to call someone. And you know
you're still talking about the body,
and it's still your body. Call the street
"Cat's Game" and the city "Red Shift." Call your friends
and they're talking from behind tents
about Cat's Game and Red Shift. How long
has it been like this, and does it mean
you do or don't get to sleep with the pretty people,
when they've all become so ungainly, so charming
and such odd things to count on?

What is there now to place yourself inside of? What
is reasonable? And would it be an ever-growing series
of larger tents, called things like Protocol
or Formaldehyde? Why is it never the rainbow tent
or the comedy tent? You try the bear mask
with a piping of cotton balls along the brow ridge.

So it seems you're suddenly so perceptive
you should maybe try your hand at some profession soon,
or game show. Begin anywhere. Walk up the street to the left,
and it's a tent in motion. A grocery list
you have to recite when you come across others. Luckily,
you don't have to know what the words mean
in order to say them, like "There are a lot more opportunities

for sensible investing," and "It's all part of the service
agreement," when they contain their opposite,
as all things do, or are said to.

Can you contain your opposite then,
and coast all the way down? And, lucky once more,
it's not a real question. And it's not
a real tent, as the weekend is almost always on its way
with its own hollow places
of easily painted landscape over crowds of people.

ON YOUR SMOOTH RIDE

It's raining on ice. And all your old enemies,
whose names you made flags from,
are someone else's enemies now,
dreaming about trouble
because trouble is fun to dream about.

They're making up
for lost time, on the rails, missing you
a little, even though they can't remember your name.

Sometimes they're sorry
about the way things turned out,
and all those old looks,
those old flags you fold and unfold
carefully. That you place in the teak dresser.

There's some truth to that, I think. But there's some truth
to pretty much everything,
on your smooth ride.

So what do you want me to say, maybe I'll say it,
as talk of light
surrounds the light around you
in the rectangle of light from the front window.

Air on fire all around you,
orange light and yellow light and white light.

THE FRACKVILLE ANGEL

All things considered, we do not
live very long. This knowledge haunts us
the way a leak in the kitchen haunts us,
or like a golfer underground—

we can hear him, we know he's there
in his knit shirt, soiled now, putter dulled
against humus and stone, keeping you
from being somewhere you would rather

be, downstairs, say, fixing that leak.
But the golfer keeps chipping away,
so that eventually all you want
is to get out of the house, get in the car

and *drive*, even if "somewhere"
looks an awful lot like central Pennsylvania:
hardscrabble mining towns,
rusted-out Chevys, some home-movie

version of *The Molly Maguires*
playing in every bedroom, every
roadside bar. At least you've left the golfer
behind. At least you're in motion.

You're feeling pretty good, actually,
which is why you stop for the hitchhiker.
He looks like a decent kid, a little
damp, maybe. God knows how long

he's been standing there on the shoulder
of Route 11. You know the stories,

you've seen the movie yourself: Now
comes the part with the flashing lights

and the police cruiser, the mysterious
telephone call and the disbelieving sheriff.
The part when one of you turns toward
the other, to find the other isn't there.

BUSMAN'S HOLIDAY

In the kitchen where the bridges
dream they go at night,
somebody is pouring a cup of coffee.

Somebody else
is pretending to be an angel.

Since none of us really has any idea
what an angel is like,
this is actually pretty easy:

You've got a lot of latitude.
Sometimes
there's a quick judgment call, like

what would an angel do

if somebody spilled coffee
on a bridge. Or
what would the rest of us do

if somebody dropped a bridge
on top of an angel.
We're assuming angels

are immortal,
but that's not the same thing
as invulnerable.

At some point, juiced
on caffeine, somebody suggests

that at least one of us
is an angel, pretending he's a bridge.
This is a difficult moment

like in the falling dream,
trying to wake up
before you hit the ground.

THE HISTORY OF ENTANGLEMENTS

You drive down the block. All the garages
are open. Fathers are working with their sons.

"I'll tell you those rock candy mountains,"
they say, as part of the speech
they cut out of a magazine and placed on the wall
next to the door to the laundry room.

On the sidewalk, we were lost,
though we only had the two directions
to choose from, so that now,
we could try a rotating circle backward,
to encompass more territory.

It was *this* father, I think. The one
with the blue shirt, in some next address
nearly spilling the interior of the house
into the yard.

Doesn't it make you happy,
driving the car through early fall,
with all these garages open. All these trampolines
in the yards.

On the next street, in the second headache
or the third headache, it's started to rain.

Perhaps this was the dog that was in that yard
that year. It has set itself up
under the maples, beneath some stones.

ELEGY FOR ROSA PARKS

Things have a logic
of their own: museums, wars,
breakfast specials.
We think of these
as little windows. When we
look through them

we see children playing
on a green lawn.
We see other windows
framing candles.
We see buses, some half-
full, others half-empty.

We build houses
with entertainment centers
and floor-length
mirrors, Formica counters
and laminate floors.

Famous cities
filled with the dead
move on
into lives we can't touch.
After a while,
we learn not to look
at fire so closely.

Things kneel and we
step into them: a film
clip, a photograph,
a hand resting in moonlight.
We adjust the equations.

We trace names
in the earth and the snow.

THE WORLD IS EMPTY & A SPLASH OF SALTS

Where you're living above a cave
and you're covered in bats,
wondering how memory works.

Is it an elevator shaking the walls?
Is it an old woman with a filing cabinet?

Or is it that we love it best
when we don't know where we are
and it's a party of some sort,
which permits you to catch several things
in unresolved bits,
like our interchangeable fathers
deep in snow.

Above a cave just like this cave,
there is a man talking about this cave,
or one just like it.

"It's much like this cave," he's saying.

"In full winter, it's good to be
above a cave." That's one option. Or,
"I am made nervous by the cave."

I am made extravagant
by the hooks along the walls, the hooks
that are made to dance as we move past them.

Presence is enough, perhaps. We can just stand here.
Maybe this is nothing like the cave,
that other one.

But perhaps I meant something else by that
in the past. Perhaps I meant,
on the verge of becoming gestural,
like overnight clouds,
I kept meaning to do something.

CANDLING THE BODIES

So our job at the hangar
was to hold each of the bodies
up to a bright light, to see

if there were any other
bodies inside.

Day in, day out
we sifted the bodies
from their crates of sawdust.

When the electricity
was good, we used a high-
voltage spotlight.
When it was bad,
we had to build large fires

and use magnifying lenses.

Mostly we didn't see
anything at all.
Sometimes, we thought we saw
another body, deep inside
the body we were looking at.

It was hard to be sure.

I remember reading in bed
late at night, when I was a child,
the way the flashlight
made a veiny map of my hand.

It was a little like that.

When we saw,
or thought we saw, a body
inside another body,
we placed that body
in a separate pile.

Someone came
in the night, every night,
and cleared all the bodies away.

ESCAPE STRATEGIES

A kind of clarity rises, like leaving a room, going
and coming back. It forms a narrative
where the goal is to count the bodies,
to make them into furniture.

And night falls where it may,
with the private lives of individuals,
where you don't know what to do next, and maybe
counting's fine, but then, maybe not,
maybe counting's a mess
and you're on the very edge of something large
rushing at you, though most of the time you know
there's nothing all that large rushing at you.

Such thoughts. And look,
he turns on his phone
and he turns off his phone. "I'm sorry,
my phone is ringing," he says.

Some people enter, some keep entering.
They're sure they're traversing a wide field. "I might die here,"
they say. Or, "My father died here."

You can count the doors
and windows. You can tell yourself
you're working it out
or that everything that ever frightened you
is on the other side of an empty cage.

THE GREAT MIGRATIONS

All afternoon we kept seeing the hands
in the distance, at the skyline
or else just a little bit above it:

great clouds of them,
like dark birds.

At dusk we imagined them nesting
in the branches of oaks,

but when we went out again, later,
we saw them
wheeling and turning

against the night sky,
or rather, their shadows,
blocking out bits of the constellations.

It was as if someone
were subtracting pieces
of all the stories we'd ever been told,

just for a moment,
just to see how that would work:

Orion without his belt,
Pisces twinless,

the Great Shopping Mall
without its parking deck or waving flag.

Frost had settled.
We could see our breaths
in the darkness.

Maybe it's time
for some new stories, you whispered.
Maybe that's what the body
was wanting, all along.

YOUR FATHER CALLING FROM THE MUSEUM

The streets wrap the house in ribbons, and for a second, we
say, "Look, I'm sorry. But I've gotten tired of my story."

And we sing a chorus of "You Don't Always Get What You
Need."

It makes me feel more pleasing to admit it.

Behind the cartoon of the pelican and the mule, the day dims
and flares as clouds pass, and we're going to imagine
friends for our children who die.

A second floor because the spring eats the way all houses are
meant to be painted and repainted.

Later impressions forthcoming: the persistent itching; the red
ropes, a balcony because it's a struggle between life and
other life, the alarm miscellanea.

A roof because everything that scared you as a child still
scares you.

And you remember suddenly that you won the lottery years ago,
and you've been rich all this time, so what's the worry.

There at the heart of the matter, it's an easy drive. No one
will wake you.

Maybe your friends, or the company you keep, maybe they
tell all, or wish to, if only someone would ask.

Restrooms, because you're hoping to look well-adjusted,
bleeding into your shoes.

Let's go back to the party, where you toss yourself or find
yourself, or neither one, in no particular order.

It won't stay like this, which is another of the difficulties
we have with photographs, as if the afflicted could jump
right in.

THE SHERPAS OF CANADA

The Sherpas of Canada
are leading you, and your automobile,
north, to a lake.

The automobile is old.
Maybe you're old, too, or maybe

you're just getting older.

On an island in the center of the lake
stands what's left
of a house.
Inside it live three little girls.

The house has collapsed,
but the little girls don't seem to mind.
The little girls
are actually dolls,
but it's possible they don't know this.

Will you be our doll,
one of the little girls asks.
She has a smudge
on her porcelain cheek,
and one of her eyebrows is missing.

What you want to say is:
I'm sorry
about the love thing, how nobody

ever quite got that right,

and for the way I treated the kittens,
and for all those bad movies.

What you want to say is:
I'm sorry,
I just can't be a doll to dolls.

Instead you find
you can't say anything. It's as if
someone had painted a fake mouth
over your real mouth.

It's cold, and the wind's picking up.
You try your keys
in the automobile's ignition.

Nothing happens.

Behind you, the Sherpas start singing.
Or maybe it's just the wind.

YOU NEED NOT BE PRESENT TO WIN

And then comes that moment in the process
when we all have to transplant live organs from dogs into cats.
There will be an exam. Or maybe this *is* the exam.

It's not the same thing as waking up.
I mean, there are similarities:
the silvery shine of the instruments, that sense of struggling
back up out of a mineshaft that's been lubricated
with mincemeat and failure, that feeling somebody is watching,
somebody who may not have your best interests at heart.

You want to find that somebody and say
Hey, let's have a beer, maybe pick up some take-out Chinese
and eat it in the park, watch the swan boats,
only you realize it's December, so there aren't any swan boats,
and anyway you don't live in that city anymore.

At some point you no longer hear the barks
and hisses and low, inhuman moans of the dogs and cats,
or at least, you realize they no longer register
inside you, in that inner part of "you"
where you're still a boy trying to put model planes together,
smashing garnets from the schisty gravel
of your great-aunt's driveway,
not wanting to get picked last for yet another team.

You want to get a good grade on the exam,
when it's time for the exam. I mean, if this isn't already it.

So you keep working, keep getting better, you think,
at this strange task to which you've somehow
been called. It's not all bad. There's waking up, and then
there's going to sleep again, and even if there's a lot of blood

and pain and waste involved, sometimes
there are these beautiful mountains in the distance—

December, for instance. The feel of cold
steel against your fingertips. The way the body exfoliates,
like wings cut from cloth or leather.
The smell of holiday cooking wafting from the refectory,
what washes easily from your chapped hands.

AND AS THEY WAITED IN THEIR BASKETS
ON THE HILLSIDES IT BEGAN TO RAIN

I meant to write "saved from drowning"
but wrote "drowned from saving"
instead. When I look up from my notebook,
I realize I am writing
once again at the desk made out of the war.

Later, after the lights are turned off,
I hear the Jake brakes of passing trucks and litanies
the crickets make. It's as if
at some point, or maybe in some other,
earlier life, they'd all been weavers, artisans of great skill,
but then, somehow, forgot how that all went.

In the fields outside town,
the crickets are trying to piece something
impossibly complex together,
only this time it's going to work, this time
it's going to be about acoustics
and devotion, rather than about covering the body.

It's the war, I tell myself—in the dream—
before letting each fragment drop.

Come down to the water, whisper the cripples
on the tall banks of the levee.
We call what we're doing dancing
because we like that word better than some other words.
It's the sort of thing a god might do,
a god in the shape of a river, in the shape of a bird,
in the shape of a bone tucked inside a scar.

MY FATHER IN OTHER PLACES

I love people. It's easy. The stars
blow through us, we write that in letters
back and forth. And at some level
everything is as old
as everything else. How you can count the stairs
all the way to the last stair, the way I might count
across these shelves to the last box,
the garage sale box
of trophies from Field Day. And how they told you
and they tell you
you have to be real worked up
to be that person. You have to want it more than they want it,
forgetting for a moment there's very little distinction
to either of us waiting in line
for a turn at the long jump. It's the second version
of coming alive. The one
where we enter these rooms they just left,
and take their seats. How they tell you
the names change, but the names don't change. They said that
because it's friendly to say, not because it
means anything, and they say that it's important
to be clear, but they say it
in the fashion of some other time,
equivalent to the carpeting
we find ourselves upon
entering and exiting. We've plenty of carpets
to wait on, as all measurements start and end
at zero, where you cross your arms over your chest,
but then you have to decide which hand
goes under and which goes over. But that's not
new. People do it all the time. How it's a warm day. A nice day.
And we enjoy it. We walk down the stairs for it.
Close up the boxes for it. It's good to do that.
It's good how we can enjoy what happens anyway.

ON THE PERFORMATIVITY OF GRIEF
AS ECSTATIC CULTURE

The curtains in the clown house were on fire again.
The city in which the clown house was situated
lay burnished in late afternoon sun.

The flaming curtains in the clown house seemed
at first merely another burnish, an extension
or intensification of that larger burnish.

We sat on park benches, which were in the park
opposite the clown house, and watched
the curtains burn. It was OK, we told ourselves,

it was entertaining, it was merely another
part of the show. Large ships drifted
through the channels of the bay. The postal

strike continued. Eventually, of course,
the fire spread to the casements, then
to the roof, and that's when we knew something

was truly wrong: with the curtains, with the house,
with the city in which we had dwelt peacefully
for so long. Maybe with each other.

We clutched at one another on the benches
as the sirens approached. *Are they in there,*
I remember you kept asking. *Are they still inside?*

ELEGY FOR HENRIETTA LACKS

Scientists have been examining
well, everything, and they report
that there is much more of you
than anyone expected.
They've tested your neighbor;
genetically, he's actually you.
So are the goldfish in the bowl,
a good bit of the food supply
and half the population of Lebanon.
You've been spreading, it seems,
while nobody was watching.
This doesn't invalidate the results
of all their recent experiments,
it simply reduces their effectiveness:
now we know the effects
certain drugs have on *you*,
the diurnal orbit of *you*,
what it means when we try
to transplant the heart of a jaguar
into *you*. Now we know exactly
how reading Arthur Miller
raises *your* pulse, if nobody else's.
The scientists are chagrined,
of course: all those hours
in the labs, all those hypotheses
reduced to a singularity.
They surround your house,
wanting to know how you did it.
They call and they text.
They demand. The thing is,
you can't really tell them,
because you weren't
paying attention: you were

humming, frying fish for supper,
and now you're everywhere,
in the hospitals, under the fingernails
of the girls at the salon,
in the factory where tennis balls
are made. You're even dead,
or at least part of you is.
They should give you a medal,
you think, as you propose
to yourself, run a marathon,
order one more round
of tests. You're their bio-Medusa,
their medical miracle. It's
enough to make anyone tired,
which is why you went
to the clinic in the first place,
the newspapers explain—
running pictures of you
smiling, your husband smiling,
your five children smiling,
all of Baltimore smiling
into the shipyards and bay slurry.
Not that it matters anymore.
Not that it did any good.

THE OVERGROWN WAR

And the buildings missed it as well, the overgrown war, the war
we couldn't find
no matter how we looked. We're missing it again
as we speak.

"Do you hear that," we say back and forth,
as it begins to sing, thinking maybe
that'll help us find it.

Later, questions begin. Which war is best for crossing,
and which for crossing back? This,
the crossing-back war, is directed at time. We say this
mostly to make ourselves feel better.

And maybe they'll find it,
and maybe I'm not there on that day. Maybe I'm off
fitting myself into this other war
I'm trying to find, and lying about the future,
the way that doesn't seem to matter,
as the lie doesn't usually end up any more wrong
than the truth anyway.

"After the bit about the leaves turning,
we will fall on top of each other," they call out
from the loudspeakers. And we know
we've left the war half done, wherever it is.

"First you're there
and then you're older," we paint on the signs,
and then on the other signs across the road
it's, "We laid there for a while
pretending we were dreaming."

Much as if that's exactly what we want to be looking for right now, so that everyone will feel welcome.

THE BIRTHDAY HAND

At first you think somebody
has sent you a birthday card
in the shape of a hand.
It's your birthday, after all.
You unwrap the package
only to feel
the texture of real skin
against your skin. It's a real hand,
you realize, and now
you're holding it.
You're not sure what to do.
There's no note, no inscription,
no return address.
The hand feels healthy
enough, you think,
though admittedly your experience
with disembodied hands
is a bit limited.
It feels supple. It feels warm.
There's no evidence of violence
in the vicinity of the wrist.
You study the hand.
Its fingernails are manicured.
The skin is smooth—no calluses.
The veins are ever so slightly
varicose. You can't tell
whether it's a man's hand
or a woman's.
You notice a pale band
on the ring finger,
as if a ring had been lodged there
for a long time, then taken off.
You check the envelope:

there's no ring inside.
Maybe the ring
was about something else,
or someone else. Maybe the ring
had nothing to do with you.

THE TOURIST

For the sake of argument, let's call this town
your town. You only have time
for two outfit changes and Jill tumbling after,
and then it's another picnic. Maybe a stoning,
if we've had time to think about whether the law,
as it exists, has principles that apply to new situations
or not, or if someone in the family has been part of the only way
this can end. Certainly, we're here under duress,
at the radio again, as if half afraid we're going to be forgiven
for something. The way a pilgrim begins
as a little puddle of mercury and a stir stick
made from whale bone, and then we're set for bar bets
and antique instrument day, where you have to hurry,
before the yeast has time to react, and to perhaps
grab a weapon of some sort, or to call in to the call-in
show. All the words there are
are sounding, and you're standing there
in colorful boxers, thinking surely this is a new
situation. "Bespeak," we call out, then, or else we just
shuffled off to Durango, dreaming of buffaloes
and whoever has the bomb this week. But what does it matter
when no one's going to hear us? How can we
avenge ourselves against the things of this world
then? All the lovers we've left in parking lots. All
the poverty classes. The dance marathons. How average
we've ended up, counting the boats
to see if the boats stay counted. And here's your map
of celebrity houses. Change the station, and this jalopy
could use some bumper stickers. We write it
on the walls all afternoon in big interlocking circles. We
go through the box of lost puzzle pieces. We brush our teeth
and they start to disappear. We brush our hair.

DON'T WEAR OUT YOUR WELCOME

He picks up a coffee cup. He puts it down.
Maybe you've understood something. All afternoon
we read headlines about the coming birds,
and several storms off and about, picking their way.

Mrs. Pettibone mentioned tea.

You never knew what to say at moments such as these,
with the day starting to fade,
and no telephone calls to break the humming
from out the hotel window. Or else you're not thinking a thing,
which is better, of course, as the potted plants need attention
and several neighbors are dying
and getting born, which you can't help
either way, but say, "I can only say simple things."

They seem to enjoy laughing, down the lobby, in their fashion,
which often resembles crying. "It ends badly
no matter how it starts,
so why not jump right in," they're saying back and forth,
and afterward, it all gets confused by maps
and various unrepresentative colors for food and cabs anyway,
so why not get distracted by something sparkly?

Right about then, Lispeth was looking straight at Ingred,
under the lanterns, with so many things left,
and so many still to go,
and only one way to count them.

"No I'm not, then," she says, and then look,
there are people all over the hotel. It breathes.

WINTER ACKNOWLEDGMENTS

"You'll like it, I know. I'd explain now,
only I haven't got any of the papers, and besides,
it would take such a long time,
and it's rather late, and I should be getting home. Anyway,
I hope we shall all take it up hot and strong."

The girls voted it a ripping idea, there
at the maiden speech fête. It was nice, they said,
but not as nice as our cheese cakes.

It makes it just like playing a game, pretending
these new ideas are old ones
or perhaps the old ones are new, depending
on our current relationship
to this clutter no one can remember accruing.

We agreed on things, even so,
and since no one has come up with a unified theory,
well, why not be agreeable in the face
of a few missing equations?

Maybe we could hire a pony.
Or a stone with a hole in it. Or a small golliwog
and a pretty statue of Venus.

The performance came to a dead halt. You
could hear a pin: all these faces
suddenly realizing the performance
had stalled. And now I can't remember a thing.

THE SOLITARY DEATH
OF THE WOOLWORTH BUILDING

after Louise Bourgeois

It's the day before a holiday
and you're out weeding the hostas
or else taking a midnight
walk through the town cemetery.
Either you do or you don't

hear the distant
howling of dogs, detonations
that must be fireworks
or maybe thunder, klaxons
of ambulances crossing the highway.

You check the roses,
which seem canker-free.
You peer over the forsythia hedge
to catch a glimpse of the ark
your neighbor
is building in his backyard.

You scan the sky.
Heat lightning, you tell yourself.

Inside, you write poems,
and then you shorten the poems
you have written.
The dead are very kind,
you decide. They let you live here
free, for one thing.

Someone's opening
a new museum downtown
about what life was like here
before, when the weather
and couture were more predictable,

before the salt ran out

and what you sewed together
came back as bodies,
immense, floppy, anthropomorphic
forms you fold and store
in your basement, attic, closets.

They're not quite as comforting
as the pets you used to have,
but they're much more manageable,
you tell yourself,

which is true, allowing
for the incessant whispering
during the dark hours
and the smell, a little like cinnamon,
a little like water rising
up through the floorboards

which you keep meaning
to replace, anyway,
with something more reflective,
something vertical,

a flagpole or a skyscraper,

something the crowds will point to
when they gather, murmuring.

THE NIGHT AUTOPSY

Things start with fire, or else with music.
Some of us are at the restaurant where the bird got in,
and some of us are elsewhere, and anyway
that was another occasion, some other evening.

Outside, crowds of young people are cheering.
They do this every afternoon here,
about this time. I hear their voices more clearly
when I open the windows, but I still don't know
what they're shouting, or to whom.

In the dream I keep having
I wind up dismantling my desk, only to find
it's constructed not of human bodies, as I'd feared,
but rather out of small slivers of glass
in the shapes of bones. Every time
I hold a fragment up to the light
I see something different: an empty sleigh
being pulled across a dark, snow-studded
landscape; a Bedouin market in ruins; two little girls
holding hands with their backs to the camera.

Maybe the crickets aren't trying
to make music. Maybe they're trying to thread
their own legs together, make something
larger than themselves. Or maybe they're trying
to kindle something, steel against flint.

After the fire, November was a surgeon's voice.
The time the bird got in the restaurant
we all thought it was funny.
There was music for the war to dance to, if it wanted.
Our faces were still painted, from the parade.

MAKING LOVE IN THE BALLOON MAZE

Our tribe had wandered
for centuries.
Sometimes we were starving,
other times we slept
on carpets woven from rabbit hair.

In a small wooden box
one of us carried a polished
brass telescope, which
meant something, we were told:

more than just a sacred
text, divided rightly at the joints.

The balloon maze
was an unexpected obstacle,
the way it blossomed
from the fields of ripening grain.
We thought we'd stumbled
upon a planet
in the act of being born,

or perhaps an elegy
for some city we'd laid waste.
Suffice to say
we heard the music

and walked right in,
past the children
who stood stiffly
at either side of the entrance
like minarets.

When we speak of the fields
of grain outside, of the blue haze
of distant mountains,
the young
grimace, roll their eyes.

It would be one thing,
the shamans agree,
to solve the riddle, to walk out
of the balloon maze
in the same way we entered,

quite another
to destroy it in the process.

Every now and then
one of the balloons gets punctured,
in the heat of passion, say.

We bury it as we would
one of our own: with dancing,
and weeping, and prayer.

IN THE LATER MEASURES

We have an emergency,
and we're taking it for a walk. We stop for dinner.

Everyone wants to pet our emergency,
saying, "How cute."

Everyone wants to tell us things
and show us pictures, thanking us for coming.

We're as tall as the trees
when the light's right.

We're tall as the garden party, where people
are falling, where people are crying out,
characteristic
of how they're supposed to react.

We take it for a walk around
the park. We feed it.

The neighborhood slows.

We have an emergency. We treat it well.

SCANDINAVIAN SKIES

One country starts out as a bank
and ends up as a solarium.
Another is a byproduct of somebody else's
experiments on bees.
Either way, bombs get manufactured

and one day someone wakes up
to find he's hip-deep
in false advertising, direct mail

piling up against the house
past the windows, funneling into the roof.

People vanish, and we say,
"Look at that antique corner cupboard,
how charming, how quaint,"

while at the same time
switching out mathematics
for yet another zombie radio station
broadcasting baking powder
and all the new names for fire.

If we rescued the guy in the house,
we'd suffer consequences:

other people, the way shopping malls
reflect the sun's investment
in consumer culture.
Nobody knew the name of that disease
when we started:

the countries doomed by obsessive
philately, the principalities of back taxes
and snow, the bake-offs
and the kick-offs and the die-offs;

the songbird extinction threshold,
the unspeakable things
some of us began to do with wolves.

It's elementary, the children whisper.
Look how far we've come.

LANDSCAPE WITH MISSING ELEMENTS

We sit through the eulogy. Bits of flowers
all over us. Little death confetti.
We wait with them
or for them.

Either way, we sit with the incantations,
proceeding to the X,
and the music is interminable, isn't it?

And the evenings
to come. And then a few more.
Maybe drinking in the parking lot.
Some greenery. Or the radio.

We could call it practice,
as it's all about being ready.

A field of people running.
Or a nest of buildings
where the winds aren't favorable,
but let's start out anyway.

The service is pleasant enough.

A feeling of wonder even, like maybe
it's raining in the mountains.

We stop for a moment to talk.

I have made mistakes.
I have turned to you
and it's been my reflection in the window.

MAYBE IT HAS NOTHING TO DO WITH YOU

You've read all about what havoc butterflies cause
from far-away places, whole grass-roots movements
on the head of a pin. It's just on the cusp,
teetering, waiting for you
to make the first move. A friend from
high school is sitting down to dinner
and you cross his mind or her mind, and then someone
you've never met sees your name
on a piece of paper. Above your name
is written, "You said this will be our only chance,
and you were right." This envelope has wandered through the
    mail
for three years, or seven, as a form of paralysis
or parenthesis, housing a bit of information outside of grammar,
as if anything can be contained. As if thinking
is part of it, where you think you're another one
of the people. You're thinking you'll keep every picture
you've ever had. You won't need to write names
on the backs. It's enough that they shine
in the light. Every flash. Every cable. So sure,
every envelope is a hand. And it's your hand. *I love my life.*
I hate my life are the same sentence. It will be our only chance,
you think. And you think you should write that down,
just once, and let it go after that. Because you mean it. Sitting
    there
in the flash of the camera, and the second flash
off the mirror. People going by. People talking.
If only they'd stop or never stop. We
had a fine evening. And yours. Yes. And what a year.
Because you don't know if you should keep it or not.
Because you don't know if you remember.

THE RADIO INSIDE YOUR HEALTH PLAN IS SLEEPING

At first you thought it was somebody else's
past life you felt skirting past the Laundromat
on your way to the public library:

the ripple effect, you know.
Then you thought maybe it was an escaped
river, a river on the run,
which made for a more substantial
romantic investment
on the part of the dieticians
on break from the hospital,
sitting on picnic tables in the shade
of a few mangy Bradford pears.

It's the sun, you tell yourself.
That, and the vegetable petroleum
applied to all the produce at the supermarket
"to preserve freshness."

What you want is a spontaneous
musical interlude, one that doesn't include
12-tone vacillations from the baseline
beepers, the chug of the jack drill
eating through pavement.

If Santa Claus is really a myth, you think,
then it's a myth with teeth
filed to points. It's a biker myth,
built on leather and speed

or at least the *ideas* of leather and speed,
which is what you tell the doctor
when you come to in the emergency room.

It's oddly quiet, you think,
shifting a little in your hospital gown
so that you can see what the nurse
holding down your shoulders looks like:

a male nurse, as it turns out,
wearing a birthday hat carelessly on his head,
a streak of blood digesting his scrubs

into that pop song you can never
quite remember, the one with the perfect
guitar hook, the one they never play anymore
though you keep calling and asking.

AS MASTERY DECLINES
INTO ALTITUDE AND FORGIVENESS

Another jet plane is falling from the sky
and doing it so gracefully
it almost seems to want to be
polite, not trying to get your attention,
not trying to make a statement, just giving in,
at long last, to gravity, or maybe

distracted, momentarily, by a flicker
in the landscape, wanting to see something
close-up that's not an airport.

You're either sitting at a patio
in view of the falling plane, or else
you're sitting at a patio somewhere else,
eating a sandwich or about to eat
a sandwich, or maybe you've just eaten it,
are waiting for your check or your date
to return from the bathroom,

and you think how almost tender an airplane
is when it falls, how it seems to fall
slowly, as if gravity were actually a film,
one you've seen hundreds of times
but now, in slow motion, you catch little bits
you hadn't noticed before,

the peculiar blocking in the casino scene,
the continuity error in the museum.

You think, something's funny here.
You think, the trees must know a lot more

about the serial bafflements
mercy throws in invention's face.

You've seen this one before, but
that doesn't prevent you from praying
just a little, before you rise from your table,
before you take your lover's hand.

FLIGHT OF THE DEMOLITION FACTORY

We'll sure miss the old place,
I guess. No, really. The voices, as they go,
are nearly intoxicating,
and we think about it every now and again,
with the cocktails and hostile witnesses,
as they fly over our heads,
barely glimpsable through the glowing windows
and Halloween candy.

It's wrong to say so, I know,
but I want to be there. I've always
wanted to be there,
though a fundamental lack of examples
dogs the project, so that it's not a real distance,
but a closed set of variables
within which we sweep little piles of pictures
drawn by children.

The people there know what to say at all times,
no matter what the view out the windows,
some star-struck pedestrians
along the sidewalk
measuring off the distance
from one side of the avenue
to the other. Some practice for the emergency,
some look for a discrepancy
in the accounting procedures,
and there we are, look at us, asking if somewhere
people still do such things.

It's easier if you find the surprise switch,
and the building rises. And how nice
that is, where certainly

we're older, and occasionally
want to break for sandwiches,
and say, "Yes, Frackville, or anyplace
we've already been,"
but even so, we keep the registry book close
as it keeps flipping open to the same page
whenever we put it down.

AROMATHERAPY IN THE AGE OF NEW FORM

Sure, the idea of curative smells
makes as much sense as, say, cancer
does, the body mutating against itself.
When you stop remembering
the signature equations
emanating from the military beacons
it becomes easy to feel attractive
all over again, to be the first
to blood the boar, to order absinthe
and lift its obsidian mule
to your chapped lips.
Melancholia, melanoma, Malathion
you repeat to yourself, sinking slowly
beneath the other customers
you've imagined in this bar,
the off-duty bailiffs, the legal aides.
The reason houses are built foursquare
is the tenacious verticality of trees
which keep surprising us
in their capacity for altruistic
self-destruction. It's true, René Char
fought for the Resistance,
committing his romance with the nation
to memory's vellum asylum.
We read him in the shadow of
Desnos, Keats. If you offered me a gun
I would know just what to do
with my medical history
masquerading as this twisted menorah.
It makes a difference
whether you evade the tolls
out of mere boredom or a more particular
will to power, to resist constraint.

Atalanta used the gods' own fruit
to speed her lover, which meant
slowing herself
so that she could give birth,
later, to an opera. I don't
want to get too serious about this:
I had to use Wikipedia to remind myself
who Atalanta loved.
His name was Melanion,
or else Hippomenes—like everything
at myth's distance it's hard now
to be sure. All the crows
lift from the power lines at the same
moment, circle the same maple
as if some secret telepathy were at work.
You see those shiny things along the road
where they've sprayed for weeds:
Chekhov's ghost sighting
down both barrels. Experience
glances off the physical
and we call it "ivory," "chocolate,"
"napalm," "brie." We stop to pick it up.
Simone Weil had some ideas
about freedom, too, you know; they
killed her. Studies show
if I draw myself making friends
with my disease I'm much more likely
to transcend it, so I do. Then
I burn the drawing. It smells like gasoline
and cinnamon. I cross my forehead
with its residue of waxy ash.

EVERYTHING YOU KNOW THAT ISN'T TRUE

This is a cut-out doll. Let's name it your child
and place it on the windowsill. You can sit next to it
while you crack your knuckles.

You can place it up against the window
so that it looks as if it's running across the yard.

It's a more recent idea,
full of reports you must read out loud
over the telephone to strangers.

The cars moved slowly back then,
and you could hear them from a great distance,
filled with ice cream trucks.

"I moved very quickly back then," you should say. Or,
"I didn't think a thing!" Maybe you didn't see a thing.

"Have I misunderstood faith," we ask.
It's like waking up to a kitchen
full of open cupboards, asking,
"Where did the child go?"

How secretive we were
when you were five. The ice cream truck you could hear
around the corner, blindly, and you had to run
into the street.

"I have hidden something in the kitchen"
is another example. For a map, we say we used to run fast,
so fast we had to leave it there.

I jump over the bushes and come down on both feet,
and rise to the sound
of traffic. When your mouth opened it was sirens.

II

IDEAL BOATING CONDITIONS

You open the box and see yourself staring back.
"Cool," you think, and then you realize
it's just a mirror at the bottom of the box.

The wind shifts. The little boats go this way
and that in the harbor. You watch them.

Somewhere on board each of the boats
is a mirror, from which you watch yourself
watching the boats. The self you're going to be
sends postcards back to the self you are now,
only the self you are now won't get them
until it's too late, until you're different.

You think the part of you that is out there,
in the harbor, must be happier than you are now.

There's this wedding you're missing,
or this anniversary. The music cycles backward,
past Chopin, Bruckner, Buxtehude even.
See, this city isn't even built yet.

You want to use every word you hear
as a verb: "neon," "medical student," "Talmud."
"Persimmon." "Volkswagen." "Aramaic."

You read the postcards one by one
like cadavers inside of which cloudy coils
of ocean have just gone missing.
A gentle breeze off the water ruffles your hair.

Someone's excavating Troy, someone's
living there—the little shops, the excise tax,

a furnished room near the college,
baskets of blue eggs in the marketplace.
The searchlights launch themselves into the void
music's left, hatchlings on the riprap.

The you that's on the boats misses the you
that's here, with the box. You understand this
much. Someone else's Troy is burning.

PHARAOH'S DAUGHTER
(CHAGALL MOTION STUDY)

You're going there. And you know
there are ways to do it, because you've read
the newspapers, the travel advisories,
seen the timetables and the photographs.

It's Portland or Eugene or else
some new form of German unforgetting.

In the pewter tenements nostalgia
is secretly forging all the celebrity careers
you won't know about
until later, until it's too late.

You're just one of the stones in the Capitol,
or in the alleys leading to the Capitol.
The website says, "Remember,
not all animals needed to be full-grown,
not every variation of every genus."

The website says, "Consider all the facts,
and it makes a lot more sense than
the little 4-animal arks you see
in pictures and toys." 1.5 million cubic
feet of space. 40,000 animals.
Special restrooms for the handicapped.

Because everything is still evolving.
Because here is your gold star.

New shops open in Czernowitz,
in Terezin: a post office, a discotheque.

This is how we know the model's
built to scale: little Braille murders.

So much is water to the human body.
Think of all that beautiful jewelry.

YOU'LL GET NOTHING MORE
FROM ME TODAY, SHE SAID

And then she hid herself in the public works project services
for the indigent. We missed a lot back then,
on account of all the accounts they were telling us of the war
and who she was sleeping with, and what they were doing
    there.

Yalla yalla, they said, meaning the next wave
will be different than this one. In that way
it's like the last one,
the great masters intimated. Every once in a while though,
we make some clever comment,
and that pleases us, in some quasi-worried manner
over coffee, out on the porch, only to be harried by a cardinal
for the rest of the morning. Sent undoubtedly
by the pope, you think.

All points cluster at the same point, and are just to say
those were the grand salad years,
as we were practically swimming in the stuff back then
in the perfect replica of a town square
where sometimes we'd find old coins. And sometimes
we'd spend them.

What she meant by anything else she said, we'll never know,
as it hovers back there at the harbor
with all those other things left undone
that had to be finished by others
or left unfinished,
which becomes a kind of completion
that one can hope for, but without ever knowing,
so that whatever it is now keeps tapping at you

with a little stick of bent wire and rubber bands
that begins to feel like comfort, something
you can call your very own.

APOLOGY RE: THE SECOND VIENNESE SCHOOL

Everything takes a couple of shots today: Schoenberg,
the plumbing, the heat refraction index, the angle of incident
at which a body falling at such-and-such a rate of speed
strikes another body, falling at a related but not identical rate
    of speed,
such that you return from the recital at a much later date
    than you expected,
after the interviews are over, after the last of the rebels
appeared on television, after the mockumentary on
    liposuction
was denounced in the media and all the little boats drew back
    into the harbor
you're thumbing past in a glossy magazine ad
for geriatric care you hope you never need. The nurse says,
"You should experience a slight stinging sensation," and you
    do.

You wanted to tell some friends about what the
melting ice caps mean to the phytoplankton on which
some of the regional megafauna must depend, somewhere
    down the line,
but all circuits are busy and the city itself is out
christening a burn unit with some new capital accumulation
paradigm. The nurse says, "Look at this photograph," and
    you do.

Your friends write to you with the news that they want to
    board
the beautiful ship, the one hovering just offshore in the
    magazine photograph.
You think this is your friends' way of saying, "We're getting
    older,

just like you," only objects are almost never closer than they
      appear
and anyway physicists are still debating the precise velocity
at which everything in the universe is speeding away from
      everything else.
The nurse says, "When you hear the beeping tone, press
      ENTER."

A box arrives with your name on it, and a hood inside.
You're not sure whether you're supposed to wear the hood
      now,
or maybe later. Maybe it's for someone else. You dream in
      Spirographs
that move slowly from text to text like prisoners circulating
within a system of domestic incarceration, Big House, Little
      House.

The nurse says, "Close your eyes. Can you feel the wave
      motion?"
And you can: a gentle rocking. It would be pleasant
if you weren't in the hands of something so much larger than
      music seemed
to be, larger than the real estate market, larger even than
      Germany.
We go to sleep in its arms and it sucks the ghosts out of us,
      one by one.
They like it there, they tell us. They're hanging out with your
      friends
and getting a lot of sun, and there is something like dancing,
only it isn't really that, you'd be terrified if you knew what it
      really was,
but no matter, everyone's on time there, everything's fine.

TRENTON AUBADE

The plow is made entirely of chocolate, which is why
it goes so easily through the window, and why the little girl
throws flowers after it, one, two, a whole bouquet.
Since Dali's film is in black and white, we can't tell what
    color
the flowers are. Maybe it's not important, maybe

the bridge cables were designed by Roebling
as a way of finding more things to do with iron and steel
and more money to charge, more people
to sell them to. Your grandfather's birthdate is incidental
to the larger enterprise on which the caption rests,

running the camera lens slowly along the length
of a single corn shuck. *Texture, plexure, vesture*
chant the realtors and the philatelists from their box seats:
it's the same plot as baseball but less showy,
meaning you don't have to manufacture a new class identity
in order to alert the populace to what the hero is wearing.

The hero isn't conscious of any haptic sensation
in his paralyzed limbs, but that doesn't mean there isn't any.
At altitudes such as this even birds can't contain
the grammar of "continues" vs. "quite lovely,"
a vigilance the sea keeps aspiring through its illusion
veil of gravity, chitin, and salt. Fast-forward, and

all we can recover from the darkened autoclave
is a pair of hands throwing music at some shadows,
sapphire unemployment data MapQuest hasn't photographed
yet. You can walk across, only you don't want to.
At some point you realize you *are* one of what the bone people
call "everybody." There's ample oxygen for this,

a lot of nothing that could explode at any moment
now that you're almost arrived. It's New Jersey. The operators
can't help it, they're waving, they're on the train,
they're crying into their electrocarbinated window displays
but they are standing by, standing by, standing by.

YOUR FATHER SEEN FROM SPACE

It's been a difficult day at work. He's tired.
What we continue building
overtakes us, he says. Just as every time we reach out,
the ground's always there
so that people will have something
to keep them occupied
while they wait for their numbers to be called.

Dinner on the patio sounds nice.
He stands there a moment
in the doorway
holding a plate.

We send postcards to ourselves,
several a day, in fact, just to say that
fathers can lift you and carry you.

Fathers place you in your bed
when you fall asleep.

Maybe at the end we can sum it all up
in such a way that it'll be remembered
as completed and coached along.

He's making a phone call.
He doesn't look happy about it.

Certainly someone
should have mentioned something about this
to us before now, how the judge
is the judge's chamber
and the cheerleaders exhaust themselves
at the rally, as a form of geometry,

so that we can get to a place
where we can say
yes, finally, just before the fiery crash.

ODE TO LYNDON BAINES JOHNSON

If one could step outside *meaning* long enough
to consider, say, this Edward Gorey graphic
alongside this photograph of an apple and a typewriter
in a small-town shop window. What is it
about the German language you don't understand?
There's a ballet performance, and either
you're there, in the audience, or you watch it
later, on DVD or television. Or else you don't,
and anyway that nice new restaurant down the street
isn't open for lunch, not on Tuesdays.
We fold the Midwest up like the map it is
and stuff it inside a schwa, from which anyone can see
all the faithless self-indulgences of broadcast news.
I'm not so much interested in "what race is telling us"
as in where race goes when it walks in its sleep.
Even if the results aren't admissible in court,
I'd still like to imagine a place where we might say
Yes and mean not only *Yes* but also *How do we know*
and is it possible to order a contract without
a side of videotape and poison. One morning the man
who taught you phonics is alive, then he's dead
inside a starling education initiative
masquerading as performance art. I start
listening to things that are vertical
long enough for me to stand very close with one ear
up against them: flagpoles, buildings, trees.
It's like dancing, only very slow, a small New England
congressional delegation in favor of more
postal holidays. Our stake in the common
milk supply is small, but without it
somebody would already have fallen in love
with the wrong sportscaster document. In Vegas
it's existentially correct to let other people tie your shoes

to low-hanging power lines. There are grants for this
is what I'm saying, and more of an audience
than for beluga caviar or warmed-over Balanchine.
I want to find new reasons to register
with the government, or a new government
to register with. Or just a new DVD
that can double as extra postage, for when the rates
go up again, and those Amish kids still hiding
in the Iowa cornfields come out
and we take them to the farmers' market
and buy them Pepsis and funnel cakes
from Buddhist vendors who want to star in vegan musicals
about *Zeitgeist,* about populism, and how
one definition of a ghost is someone or something
that isn't breathing while it talks to you—
this poem, for instance, we know it's not human
but we're not scared, I mean I'm not scared,
look at the patterns the Japanese cherry blossoms
make in the reflecting pools. Isn't this
what we were almost talking about, a new way
to spend capital, a new pleiade,
the Lincoln Inaugural, Snowmass, Cannes.
Jenny Holzer has designated the swine flu
a national historic landmark, but I'm not frightened.
The apparel industry reports a slight drop
in summer sales owing to all this outrageous
sunlight. It's so beautiful, all this left-over
pharmaceutical packaging on the grounds
of the abandoned Boy Scout camp, polydactyly,
pleather, even the dents in the hood of my Subaru—
so beautiful, the big dams, the hash browns.
Red matter. The Corn Palace muffled in snow.

ELEGY FOR THE DEVELOPING STORY

In the bone trees, they split us into two groups:
the mosquito group and the feces group. None of us
fared well. "See how it all fits
into the plan," they asked, "how the stooges of machinery
	hover
at the cornice, holding scrolls with the names
of who will be chosen next? Well,
we don't either, and it's starting to wear us
into shapes, like a baseball glove or the postal service."

And with that there was a light breeze
and the candle caught the curtain, solving most of our
	disagreements
for the rest of the city maintenance cycle. I went by
her house, and she wasn't there. So I decided
to move in and wear her clothes, read her copy
of *The Potty Book for Young Professionals*.

It was somewhere between charming
and wearisome, how it's not fair to call the players late
on the night before game day, and say, "I love you
in the summertime, because all rhythms
come from the body," though it's true, or true enough,
that we are undone by the memories we don't have
of the first day, what we might have said
that got everything started, and how we looked
in the uniforms, under the bone trees, feeling much better
than we did before. Feeling pretty good, in fact.

WOULD YOU LIKE TO TRY
ONE OF OUR SPECIALS

When I was young, I called it my childhood,
and it can't be repeated because it was only a kind of tone
    maybe,
and situationally bound to the very people who were there—
not that you can't try, and maybe even to better results,
the way different singers take a go at the same song until it
    starts to feel
less like a song and more like a tree where one can build a
    fort
and drop water balloons on hapless pedestrians
who venture too near the tire swing.

It was that summer where you had some glass
that you might keep filling and it would just keep getting
    taller,
the eternal glass that means you can love as many as you find,
in any way you want, and there are never any questions,
just offers of help arriving night after night, cheerfully
    banging
at the door with a red ribbon and travel toothbrush.

"I will love old pictures of you," we say, "but I will love
old pictures of me best," as some other form of thinking
where we're outlasting predictions our friends made
from the railing of the cruise ship as it spilled out confetti
and early dinner specials. And behind the people
who have stopped to watch are more people who continue
unaware of all of this, and behind them, farther down the dock,
are some people who have stopped to watch something
going on over there regarding which I have no information.

And still the photographs come to us like clouds
where we can lean back and make of things
as we will. It left us all there watching the highway,
where there seemed to be roughly equal numbers of people
heading west as east. And then the penny drops. Yes,
isn't that something, though the thought doesn't help us
a bit. Just more shadows behind a rippling waterfall.

LIMITED TIME OFFER

The line runs through the hotel lobby, then extends past the
    pool,
and down and around the graveyard. The pool
looks nice. Some manatees
are performing. There's a little island in the center
with monkeys. "I can still remember the floor plan
of that house in Amarillo,"
the person beside you says. "I'm sure it's still there,"
he adds. I'd like to think it's still there, anyway. That
would bring some elegance to the equation.

The manatees wear little pink tutus and the monkeys
wear little red hats. We're leaning with or against each other,
as the line extends to the cloverleaf. We bring all the rocks
we can carry, and make little piles
when we get too much. Then we start over. The sweet smell
of a brand new day. True,
but no matter what the resemblances we undertake
there will never be a final correspondence,
despite the lists we pass back and forth
of the living and the dead, and the in-between.

It's said the line was seen in Westminster once,
where it got tangled with other lines. But so many things
    could be true
about losing touch, and having this be it, blinkered by where
we came from, but as there were two ways about it,
we found our noses a little off to the side of the grindstone
where there was a comfortable divot
within which we could rest a bit and introduce ourselves
to those around us.

And then it came time for us to find chairs
as the music stopped, and the dwarf with the garage door
      opener
was looking off toward the casinos,
pretending darkness. A few old-timers still meet there
with their checkerboards and little pieces made of filed bone.
      "We're
bone workers," they say, and the air brings a bit of dampness
as the line extends through the sand traps of the golf course
which stand there like a new idea, one you've just thought up.

CAN'T YOU SIT STILL FOR ONCE

Today's kite day in the park. The nuns
will be there. And the bankers.

There will be a wedding. They put out
fold-up chairs. There will be a little band
of children.

We like to sing the songs, too. We've
brought our flutophones
and fold-up music stands.

If we listen well, we can hear
the buildings down one side
of the street
and up the other.

We never knew the buildings
could be so pretty.

It helps us keep time. It's important
to keep time, with the kites there above us.

It's important to have something to do.

DIFFERENT FROM WHAT
YOU BARGAINED FOR

You go to the apple stall in the supermarket
for some apples, only they're all coated in chrome
this time. You buy some apples anyway,

noting that chrome-covered apples are heavier
and cost more than regular apples did,
or do. On your way out you ask the produce man
"What's up with the chrome-covered apples?"

but he just shrugs, as if to say *I do what they
pay me for.* It's as if you've just come in second
in a race you didn't know you were running

on account of having been held up
in line at the library, or the acupuncturist's.
You think, These won't taste as good as the apples
I remember from when I was a child.

But then, you think, even if they weren't
coated in chrome, they wouldn't taste as good.
Outside in the afternoon sunlight

the hearses are circling the playgrounds again.
The playgrounds themselves are empty
but it makes you feel safer, just walking past:

How bright the teeter-totter and the jungle gym,
the chain-link fence and the Bradford pear.
How heavy the shoes you find yourself carrying
in what had been your other, free hand.

THE CARNEGIE SYSTEM

Another hearse parks in front of the library
and you think, "Whatever happened to all those nuns?"
You used to see them pretty much everywhere,

in the train and the bus stations,
in the hospital waiting rooms, at the library of course
on afternoons when the carpet mills weren't running
and everybody else's fathers were slugging

doubles over at the county park. I mean,
you've done your homework, you know all about
Vatican II, and what happened to the honeybees,
and which mid-state secessionist organization
is most likely to be financing its own secret militia.

You remembered your mother's birthday
and even your sister's wedding anniversary
which didn't really matter, since she's been divorced
for going on two years, but never mind,

it's the principle of the thing that counts,
namely that when you set the poor in rows
and make them sing, there must be someone on hand
to take down the names and field measurements,

someone to hold the hands of the wounded
as they pose on their stretchers for the cameramen,

someone to kick the tires and polish the chrome
before the door on the driver's side opens
and you find out which story it is you've been reading,
whether the hearse has come to pick up the body
or whether there's already a body inside.

BOX WITH NOISE ELEMENTS

At some point the wind always shifts suddenly
and the gust carries off small dogs
past where the king is caught in the tree
dancing along the edge of the roof. It's been nice,
and now we're applesauce.

Further postcards in the gift shop include
paintings of barges and counter girls waving
from ferries in New York harbor. We take two
of everything, and carry them outside
hoping for kites.

While falling, all you want to do is fall, they say,
sounding like all those children's stories we hid in a shoebox
under the floorboards, so we'd have something
to find someday
when perhaps we could explain them. We left detailed notes
before we moved, with Xs
and dotted steps.

Such things always start out as a memory
but end up as a question. It's no wonder we lilt
when we meet in doorways, only to bump into each other
and get turned around so that we go back the way we came,
spending the rest of our lives where we just were
thinking it was where we were going,
with the wrong children,
and feeling something's not quite right
about the wedding anniversaries. That's it,
isn't it? The story of the girl
in the woods? The darkness of the trees?

HALLS OF FAME II

Later, after the tourists have disappeared
and the gift shop has closed for the weekend,
it feels good to wash the blood and sawdust
from the working surface, although you have to use
a special oil, which makes you cough.

The stones in the chapel are slick with it.
The robins that alight in the courtyard glint with it.
It makes them fly more clumsily
but otherwise doesn't seem to harm them any.

You want to call out to the neighborhood children
who have just emerged from their hidden forts
and army tents, to warn them, but
something seems to be wrong with your throat.

They play all the games you used to play—
softball, tag, jacks—only they play them better.

In the pageant, you were some landscape
the cavalry rode in to save: hills, a few dull
buildings. A stream and some manky pines.

You wish you would have defended yourself.

All over the neighborhood, televisions
are turning themselves on, electric toothbrushes
and Waring blenders. All that energy
must come from somewhere, you understand.

It's safe to go out now. That's what we fought for,
and why the money feels good in your hands.

HOW ARE THINGS IN GLOCCA MORRA

Thank you for asking. The stones of the capital
are being used to make little figurines
of dancing children.

My pretend name is Noah.

We see paintings of trees and lakes we thought about marking
or remembering,
but what's the use? The market's tomorrow. There will be alleys
to rummage, groups to have sex with.

The empire waist is back.

I feel almost overjoyed at the warmth poverty brings,
and the help it affords us in the parking lot.

We might have already had this conversation,
but perhaps, as a form of nostalgia, it doesn't matter all that
    much,
the way all these things happening at once
aim to teach people how to create coherence
in their everyday lives.

We played those games ourselves, standing
in the orchard with our little baskets, as one
is supposed to do that, and later maybe
proposition someone in a park.

That's what I'll do when the accident happens,
and that's where I'll go, as there's a fire
one field over. We sit and talk about it. And we look it up
on the map which shows the troop movements,
the Xs where rain is falling.

AFTER THE WAR, THE ORCHARDS

They said plants liked music just as much as people,
so we installed transistor radios in all the orchards.

They also said something about our bank accounts,
but we didn't get that part. Maybe it was in another language,
or maybe we just weren't listening at the right moment.

We couldn't decide whether to mount the transistor radios
on poles, maybe even on the poles we'd already erected,
or whether to install them in the trees themselves:

in the branches of the trees. Or maybe we were supposed
to surgically implant the radios *in* the trees, in the wood.

We missed a lot back then, on account of all the noise
from the factories, and the stadiums, and the war.

But we had documents—I mean, after everything was over—
and stockpiles of helium and government surplus cheese.

We told ourselves we'd won, and maybe we had.
Everything we've ever broadcast just keeps beaming itself
into outer space, they say, farther and farther from us.

Look, from the porch you can see the orchards, burning.

CEDAR RAPIDS ECLOGUE

All the walls inside the detention center
are lined with old pictures of you.
When you peer into the microscope,
you see tiny images of a childhood tree fort
undulating slowly beneath the glass.
You say, I will always love
you, while at the same time reruns of
Starsky & Hutch
hurry on towards Alpha Centauri.
Inside the detention center,
Red Cross workers are teaching refugees
how to speak a language
that is you.
They're using the snapshots as visual aids.
It's about choice,
and hand-tinted photographs
of clouds taken from the window seats
of enormous airplanes.
You walk down to the far end of the dock.
You want to make a bomb
nobody will drop.
Then, you want to drop that bomb.
In the detention center,
the refugees conjugate verbs
that are you, nouns that are you
while weaving complicated oriental rugs
to raffle off during fundraising
telethons.
Teeth are the balloons of the soul,
says the fortune cookie.
You start to feel like maybe you're a song
a girl in some other town is singing.
Behind her, people line up

to stare into the sky. Look at that
plane, they are saying.
Is there enough pressure
in our tires, enough fluoride in our water?
Will we be on the six o'clock news?

ANOTHER DAY AT THE FESTIVAL

The tour guide walks up to you
and asks, politely, "Do you want to die by falling
or do you want to die by drowning
or do you want to die by burning?"

You say, I want to eat healthier foods,
get more exercise.
I want to spend more time with the kids,
thinking about the environment.

The tour guide nods, and gestures
towards the deep wooden bins
where they're throwing the corpses of dogs.
The shadows from the bins,
from what's in the bins, look just like
other shadows, you notice.

The wind is picking up again.
You can hear the stridor of the steel cables
attached to the bridge, that hold it up.

In your wallet you find photographs,
but they're all of things
you don't feel any special relationship to:
empty beaches, conveyor belts,
rice left over from someone else's wedding.

The tour guide is walking
away from you, in the direction
of the large building
to your left. You follow the tour guide.

It was a long time ago
when we began to mistake the motions
children made
for the children themselves.

Yes, you call out after the tour guide,
but she doesn't turn around.
You're running after where she used to be.

It's spring. Nobody knows where you are.

ETHEL & MYRTLE TRY TO AVOID HOW EMOTIONAL THEY GET

In the bric-a-brac of the yard, or the people across the yard,
Ethel and Myrtle are thinking it's not necessarily bad
to be completely misunderstood. Sometimes it'll help,
or at least buy oneself time, out in the middle of the ice storm
when what goes on in the minds of the possessed
is far from what the manuals project, with that if-you-could-
see-me-now thrill making way for the temperance guild
and general din of all our forfeitings and acquiescences.

I used to worry about my father, for instance, there
at the microscope, and now they're criticizing us for it,
as apparently they'd like us to have little adventures
that remind ourselves of just how sweet it is to have lived,
and how we all live again through it, and there's
some hope out there that feels like a rush of air
on the Stutz Bearcat, while we practice turning off the faucets
with our elbows. But they criticize us in such lonely,
defeated ways, it's difficult to feel anything
but sorry for them. "Be happy," we say, "don't cry."

Maybe if we lift something heavy. Maybe if we sit awhile
reading them sonnets that go, "How are you doing, Joe? Geeze,
I haven't seen you in *forever*." How maybe such questions
would help us think about things differently,
so that we might be better able to get past blaming
old pictures of ourselves—Look, we're all people no matter what,
with our mothers losing their minds in the living room
as we order pizza from the hall, keeping an eye on them
while juggling scissors. We never had a choice which door to
    knock on,
and now they're all the same, swinging outward, and then
    breaking.

CESAREAN SELECTION

First, sound is some meat the air is eating
while ants and wasps battle over what's left of your
Damascus apartment, after heavy rain.
William Jolliff has taken up fiddling
the way those old-time Quakers took up glue,
I mean, with money where their fingers should be
but that's OK, because he's from
Oregon, where everybody's faced with
all this paint layered up against the body, against
the luna moth trapped in the bougainvillea,
the viscous torso of the Sunday classifieds.
Dear Dave Smith, where you wrote
"eternal message" I read "eternal *massage*,"
which somehow seemed more in keeping
with the spirit of the thing, you know,
trench warfare, the prosthetic chins
and eyes and foreheads. The body is a mystery.
The bomb is a mystery, the missing pieces
of the shoppers are a mystery—
or maybe a mastery, which is what my own
fingers keep trying to type. Nations are so helpful
when it comes to rebuilding the doomed
oil rigs. When my neighbor died and,
later, I accidentally stepped into his dark
and otherwise empty garage, I saw a shovel
still hanging on the wall, blade pointed roofward.
Dear Universe, I am tired
of all your sanctimonious invocations
of dead jazzmen and rare earth elements, your
!Xhosa linguistics, your sappy faux Zen.
We pick up the children after soccer practice
and measure them into catalogues
where cattle are grazing our shoulders

with the blunt bullets of their bodies and
we say "How nice," we say "FWIW" and "IMHO."
Sometimes serial killers just get *bored,*
give themselves up: the lights go on so suddenly
it's as if you can see shadows
grabbing form from some larger darkness.
Last night I mistook "Charon" for "canon"
and then walked outside
to smell the lilacs, which were blooming
after heavy rain, some late Confederate victory
we could all feel good about, like
the Negro Leagues. Dear James Baldwin,
Stamford never loved me either.
In this box of books I've just found an old
photograph inscribed to me, only I have
no idea who the man is. He's waving.
There's snow on the ground, some evergreens
and what looks like a porch railing.
Immense machines revolve above us
advertising sex and long, dull novels
our president will never read. There will be
fossil fuels in the next life, only we won't know
what to do with them, how to untangle
imagery from affect. There will be more
swimming, more and better
milk. I liked the camp where the burn
victims used to go, to convalesce: small prayer
for the contact lens industry
in Afghanistan. Dear Zero-Sum Decathlon,
we left the choir robes in the forest
where the paramedics could find them.
The last of the Tuskegee Airmen
collects celebrity passports and vintage automobiles.
I heard about your brother on the radio.
Our dark toys blink up into the sun.

FALL IN ISTANBUL

You fall into a mystic atmosphere in Sultanahmet during
   Ramadan
after sunset. Before we left, we packed our little knapsacks
full of snacks and fruit. "The zoo's calling," we said
back and forth, though we weren't headed there. It's much
too full of stage stops from eastern Kansas. "Why now,"
we like to say, "when tomorrow seems such a grand
idea." We always feel the inversion of inside and outside
when we're in line at the concession stand. So now
we're someplace else, and feeling kind of cheap about it,
like we could've been better people once, or given more
to charity. "So what is Sultanahmet during Ramadan
after sunset like?" we asked. It's a little like morel hunting,
I think, with plenty of goodwill, someplace where the houses
still have coal doors to the basements, that most
have turned into little dungeons they name Americana.

My way gives way to more of my way
for the rest of the day, punctuated by moments
we went off to do some shunting. And no one knows
which direction the highway is coming from, really,
as we've gotten so turned around. In our memo books,
we wrote how thin writing was making us feel,
taking on the flavor of where we were writing from,
the little accents of the place, the pizza sauce. So here we are
worried it might be too close to figuration,
and that figuration might seem like dancing,
and that the taxi driver might call someone, and perhaps
they'd be waiting for us when we got to the hotel. We knew
we were talking too much, so we talked about it,
and that little driving trip through northern Ohio
when the lakes were in bloom and we were regular Joes.

ON A RAFT, RELAXING
INTO THE WEST, WHERE WE ARE

In South Carolina, an environmentalist
describes an audiorecording of the last gurgle
of the Keowee, before the dam was built,
as "The hair of an actual Christ"
while across the street from my house
a mortician's assistant is digging up a body
he will later rebury three graves over.
Sometimes we get it wrong the first time.
Sometimes we're out at the barn
when the prime directive comes through,
"Do no harm" or "Don't forget
to water the lilacs if it gets too dry."
We acquiesce to gravity—it's a reasonable
concession, like eating or sleeping—
only it turns out gravity's just a bargain
the earth made with its own rotation,
millennia ago. It's about neither us
nor professional basketball, which troubles
the bureaucrats in their little cubicles.
The list of acceptable two-letter words
in Scrabble continues to expand,
experts tell us, and No, things would not
have turned out differently,
or not much, if you'd managed to save
your first marriage, if the mills
were still turning out bolts
of high-quality greige, if the jugglers
had understood the heavy water
symbolism in *Moby-Dick*.
Moby-Dick means never having to say
"I'm sorry, can I have a do-over?"

to the frowning judges, to the television
audience. You're standing nearly alone
at the top of a great height
with odd shafts of fiberglass
strapped to your feet, and all this snow.
You can see the puff of your own breath
like some flag you've forgotten
how to salute, only it won't be the first
time some total stranger patted you
on the shoulder and said, "Be happy"
or "There's still time to read Shakespeare's
sonnets" or simply "Mind the gap."
Right now people are converging
on yet another island named after a dead
president with inflatable hammers.
I'm not sure how much I'm not
supposed to notice, I tell my ophthalmologist,
who nods, adjusts his instruments.
I listen to the field recordings:
the trading path crossed *here,* the oak
beneath which the treaty was signed
stood *here.* Neville Chute
imagined nuclear apocalypse so we
don't have to, is how one of my high school
teachers explained it, looking up
from a tattered paperback copy
of William Bartram's *Travels.*
All the nurses have left town
for the holiday. We arrive in the park
with our expectations intact
only to find somebody else's church group
hogging the picnic shelters, somebody else's
dogs tearing after the plastic frisbees.
And it's maybe a little chillier
than we expected, though the lilacs
are blooming, and it's difficult to feel sorry

for ourselves, or for the soldiers
in their distant bivouacs knitting flame-
proof balaclavas. Molten rock
seeps from beneath the surface of the earth
and the Hawaiians call it "a'a."
You can see it in the satellite photos,
along with Mexico City and the Great Wall.
From space the earth looks so much
like a great big *globe,* the joke goes,
covered with postmodernists in speedboats
and stray harbor voltage. We want
to get it right, but first we want
lunch, and Brylcreem, and designer
steroid injections, things that will make us
bigger, stronger, faster. Our parents,
for instance. We want them
where we can see them, hands up, teeth out.
We want them to remain where they are.

PRODUCTION STILL FROM *ADAM-12*

Wear the nicest thing you own. It will be
black or white, and clean. It will be another night
in summer.

Open your front door. It slipped,
almost imperceptibly. Black night. Every
small town.

The way bright light diffuses in darkness,
how, from behind,
it makes the figures glow.

A woman astride the garden
holding back the earth.

At some point
she walks from the garden. She
notices the walls
around the garden, their age. She
runs her palm along the living room walls
and television. The framed prints. She
turns all the lights on. She turns to the door,
slipping a little.

And all the doors of this town are open. All the people
are standing on their porches
in the nicest things they own.

Their hands are at their sides
clutching and unclutching. The crispness
of the chipped paint. The toys scattered across the lawns.

YOUR MUTUAL TRAPPIST

I can't walk outside because the rain
keeps coming down in different colors
we weren't taught not to point at.
We're told that coal consists of fossilized
houseplants, but nobody
really believes this, it's all a conspiracy
of Republican golem rubrics. I mean,
meat keeps rising up through the body
like golden antelope and we say,
"I thought the tournament was yesterday,"
we say, "Please pass the macaroni."
I hear more silence in your "towards"
than I do in the lace doilies
Art has placed over all the state park
stigmata. In the summer training camp,
there's a wall every camper
is supposed to scale, only it's so sheer
even scientists can't get a proper
photograph of it. This has something
to do with humiliation and something to do
with sex in places like Denver
where your luggage keeps circling
in its carousel, lurching against
the human inability to get physics
exactly right. According to the old story,
Exxon tried to translate "Put a tiger
in your tank" into Spanish, only it came out
"Put a prostitute in your tank"
and suddenly everyone in Mexico
was wearing surgical masks and bling
looted from elephant graveyards.
You wake up, and then you fall asleep
again. The dream reverses:

now you're a camel, now you're
the spiral jetty extending out into
the Great Salt Lake. In the photograph
of Dylan Thomas's boathouse
you can barely make out the corpses,
the gentle rocking motion of the waves
lapping the underboards.
Silence becomes another election
somebody's going to contest
because of how all the phenomenologists
mishandled the filming of the alien
abduction protest marches.
Contrary to popular belief, idle talk
is still discouraged, especially during meals.
Your uncle stumbles drunk down
a railroad embankment, only there's no
longer any railroad, just the collapse
of trade publishing as we know it.
You can read more about the controversy
at the PETA website, without which
even the Maori make no abiding
claim to the metaphysical master narrative.
When I say "I," I mean the faux
trap door at the bottom of the Voynich
manuscript. Little swallow
in the neap tide, tell me how to make
myself even smaller than this
backstage pass. We say "Gesundheit"
or "No, the other one, with the pixie
dust and the chocolate frosting."
The world ends, a little. Ghosts choose
us from among all the other
contagious microorganisms, and then
we're younger, only it doesn't
matter anymore, or not like we thought.
We wave at the canal boats. We invest
only in the most generous brands.

I'LL DECORATE MY HOUSE WITH YOU

You always needed more space, more ways to place yourself
in the drawer, with the clever folk wisdom you've learned
to side-step on your way to the pool party. They were called
the Floatie People, and were not soon to be forgotten, it says
on the back of this book you bought from a garage sale
for 25 cents. Best not to press the issue. It's nice, allowing
    yourself
not to press the issue, and not to need to save anyone,
and then making it to the pool party, as a nice place
when you'd really like a nice place. And some nice people,
where it looks just like anyone else's house, with predictable
frosting. Rosaries draping from the trees, let's say. And let's say
some gold choirboys in the garden next to the chrome
flamingoes. A place you can relax and be the kind of person
who says, "Make way for the tonic full of gold flakes and
    nutrition,"
and then goes to stand on the street waiting for the marathon
to pass, wispy and notional, like a marked deck, but one marked
with helpful, friendly things, and everyone's hands
where everyone else can see them, yes, and children outside
jostling at the bedroom windows. It was then we found a
    fulcrum
large enough, and the rest of the day was a breeze. Just
don't let my fiancée find out. Things would be complicated,
and then some blood pudding and blood sausage,
followed by blood Jell-O and blood salad. Even so, the houses
just stand there as you run past them, until you get to the
    point
that it's you standing there and the houses are running
into the past, as an alternate ending for everything but you,
the kind of luck you've always wanted, no longer nearly so
hermetic, like when the spies find each other on a busy street,
in their identical capes and hats—one in black,

one in white—and they exchange their bombs, and we're
all back at the pub to laugh about it and ask absentmindedly
about your aunt, I think it was, or maybe your cousin. What
was her name again? And then we invent something
for the dashboard that replicates the horizon, and we go for a
    drive.

THE APPLE IN CHROME

It's time for a caveat, and some filling in of the colors,
especially those representing sky, and the way a stitch in time
    is different
than fixing something that isn't broken.

And when I turn to speak to you,
it's not you, and that was all just something that painted the
    windows
in 1981. It was gray. And then it was the porch as well.

Excuse me, there are many more unremarkable things to say,
and roofs to place over our heads while sitting there
holding this apple up to the light.

We like it this way, as the room is reflected, and us with it,
but more vibrantly, crisper, so that everything
takes on a pleasing shape we've risen to fill.

IF I DIE BEFORE I WAKE

It was a messy waft from the lake, and the leather picnic tables
were causing a stir. Even so, we were coming down
with a plan, as that's the sort of thing one's supposed to come
    down with
after standing out in the weather with several piles of odds
and false starts from the summer training camp. We took
    some rain,
even though we didn't know what to do with it (perhaps it fits
into the overall theme, the vision, per se,
but I can't see how it works into one's coffee
or schadenfreude) or even if it would prove helpful—

This is a growing region, but there are others too, regions
and examples of regions, where we find them playing with
    puppets
or putting puppets in cases, like this region here,
where they make everything into planters. This one
was a motorcycle gas tank. This one
a puppet diner over coffee. It saves us the trouble of choosing
between our babies, as they say. Well, they now say it
differently, of course, and they mean different things by it
as well, so it's no matter. And besides, there's plenty
of not getting there one can accomplish
on one's very own porch. There's no real need for the sudden
onset of credit applications and rhubarb futures
to dissuade us from this child's chalk drawing on the sidewalk
of a sea monster on a Tilt-A-Whirl.

It seems that no one has any time for it anymore,
saying there are further levels of rhubarb at ever smaller
scales, so that, if we could just figure out how to get there,
and what to do with it, we'd be set. What we need
is a theme song, as there's no end to the possibilities for everyone

who's ever dreamed of riding camels into cities
in the middle east after sundown, carrying banners that say,
We Come In Peace. For Now. A place where confidence
is better than a plan anyway, and the future hangs there
like a glistening and eternal Colorado. I've always liked
    Colorado.

YOUR HANDS AS THE THIRD LAW
OF MOTION

The clocks of Pangaea never run backward, true, but sometimes
they go forward in pleasing, sparkling ways. The shrubbery
that was rather unsubstantial now looks like Lincoln,
and people are lining up wanting tickets and a look
at your herbicide, even if all your ideas are smaller now,
including the ones for the backyard Ferris wheel
and corn maze. It had to do with your uncle,
and now we all love the same animals. The platypus, the yak,
the manatee, and the effervescent forts they make
in the camp fitness yard, begging you to stay away from home.

Things are going on there, unlike here where everyone
has stopped in mid-stroke, even the fire in the hearth,
the choir in mid-lunge, the lovers grasping the porch rail
with everything they have, as the princess lies waiting
for some light molestation from a stranger, like when
you're in a crowded theater and something you say
sotto voce sounds like "fire," and the next thing you're able
to define clearly is filled with forms, and stories you make up
from glancing over the detective's left shoulder, laconic stories,
like the ending of some movie you didn't get to see,
but of which you had this clear vision.

Now the fields are filled with wind farms, and we're worried
we might have to start rationing weather. It certainly
seems to be calling out to be done, or to have a song written
about it being done. We should have brought some
      instruments
or taken some lessons, or understood music better. Some idle
practicing that could remind us that perhaps we should have
had children. But there's always something we were

meaning to do that we forgot to do while power washing the deck or picking up the pool passes. So maybe we did have children after all. Maybe that's what all these rooms are for.

THE OTHER PALACE

At the other palace
your laundry is already done,
pressed and folded
in hampers of polished teak.

At the other palace,
your bedroom overlooks
a small lake,
replete with swans.

You look for your name
along the long wall.
You try repeating
other people's names.

You wish you were
at the other palace.
Of course, you also
wish you were
younger, stronger, thinner.

At the other palace,
there are models of couples
dancing, singing
in wax, and better parking.

You wait in the line
by the rose windows.
Planes keep landing,
and taking off.

Your hair looks different
today, someone says.

You wave at all the people
lost in the forest.
The little lights
from the guard towers
are too numerous to count.

STOLEN CRUTCH, WRAPPED IN YARN

Dear Children of the Air,
I have bored myself with poems.
I cannot abide
the ambrotype you've chosen
to represent South Ossetia
in this year's biennale.
The blues band my friend fronted
was no good, even back
when it was good to be no good,
so let us pretend to forget
that time we spent in Oakland,
or was it Biloxi.
Let us forgive one another
the thefts or more principled
appropriations
of certain small, valuable
kitchen appliances.
Let us conscientiously erase
our names from the great
Book of Stains.
We can recycle the trophies
or else just send them
to the landfill
along with all that awful
public sculpture.
It's difficult to let go,
but without our cooperation
global warming
is never going to get anywhere
and besides, I'm exhausted
by shapes and color.
Dear Dreamers in the Apple Tree,
come down now.

Drink your juice
from its little glowing boxes.
There is nothing to be afraid of:
the mechanical systems
inside the brush arbor
have been sanitized for your
protection, the war is a Möbius
and my word processor can
suppress footnotes.
Mary Steenburgen is no longer
your surrogate Christ.
Once, setting fire to the prairie
meant "come down
to the water." Let's
televise the imperfection,
herd the tourists
back into the museums
which are, after all, now built
entirely of glass.
So that we know what it is
we're looking at. A child's ball,
a golf club. It is not a
physical sensation.
Dear Costume Drama,
I want to see you one more time.
Cut the cord. We can read
the diary later,
invent new holidays.
The world is part November.
I'm sorry:
when I let the dogs out,
they ran wildly into the snow.

YOUR REPLY IS NECESSARY

How you can lose or win perhaps, without even
entering. And that's it. That's the punch line. In order
to know the joke, you have to wait on news
from outer space, honing a revenge fantasy in the coldest place
in you, while the joke hunkers in Chambersburg, and then
    Wednesday
in Pottstown. Then back here Thursday through Friday
to get ready for the June program in Berryville,
and then later in Lancaster, as more examples that we each have
a place in the universe, and that all paths are just about
equally trod. *There's No Time Like Some Other Time*,
the signs read in one of the cities. We showed them
the door. They liked it very much. The object of our trip
was to arrive, casting about, as always, for a way to end things
into some neutral experience of that city where
there are no mimes, they say, only people in glass boxes
that grow or shrink. And people endlessly going up
and down ladders or stairs. They say they do it because everything
adds up to souvenirs, or that everything is a machine
one can count with (or to begin counting, for the really large
categories), which helps us all in the collective. They each carry
a pen and a pencil, and say things like, "What else
do we need to remember to pack?" One must forgive them
for continually pulling that rope, they don't have pop music,
which is too depressing to describe, though the letters
keep arriving, saying, "We love art." They say
it's urgent, and that you must reply with opening lines
from famous novels, and all you have is this list
of dying words of famous men. Maybe they will work,
and maybe some novel could begin, "It is well," or "I must
sleep now." It's a sort of reply anyway, as most people
only really want to know if they shall be happy,
and that hopefully poor Nellie will be taken care of. The mail

comes at noon, and it's almost noon. Go look. Maybe hold a cup of coffee. Sometimes that makes all the difference as you cross over the river and into the trees.

BECAUSE IT'S BETTER NOT TO KNOW

And we never did hear tone, with the rush of air
all around us as the sky fell.

And then you realize it's not the sky. It's
never been the sky. It's you. That's what they meant
when they said we get through most things
by not thinking about them,
except when we have the deniability of a funeral
or a bit too much wine, mesmerized
by a line of cars out there shimmering
at the horizon line.

While falling, we've plenty of time to think,
and to practice that trick
where you grasp your feet behind your back
and steer toward a small lake or circus tent.

This is a country of small lakes
and circus tents,
at various heights. So we're in luck.

You can think of it as two chambers, a filling chamber
and an active chamber, so that there are two ways
to be ill-prepared for any circumstance,
and the circumstances are all about hearing tone
in oblong numbers and triangular numbers
that somehow mean people.

You're one of them, you think,
and you're surrounded with others
over the small lakes and circus tents.

YOUR COSTUME DRAMA IS FALLING

"I used to be a blues singer," we say, because that's
what we've practiced saying, which is the same game
but with a different point, the way cheerleaders
wander the gardening center, and an artisan sits there
crafting trophies, dreaming of a lost willow peck,
each loving the moment for its own particular
pantomime of lifting and relaxing, until each reaches
the answer that says, "Sure, this way, but sideways
would also work. And hooray, of course, and is this
what it feels like to be awoken while sleepwalking?"

Why not see the world, or at least a quick stroll
through Burbank? We already tried a game of hot
or cold, but as everywhere was growing hotter,
we got lost in our own relative warmth, and could only
find the mall and some tourists. And each of us
that figures into the equation becomes also the variable
too unimportant to mention in this other equation
across town, and so we have to go and be the president
of this tennis court as well as the one who stays behind
to swab the fender skirts of passing financiers who just
lost small fortunes on the second match, bothered
by none of it for once, as it all seems equally right
and wrong, and being exhausted seems a great reason
to fall asleep, so you do, with a little shelf of tennis balls
to remember back when news from the afternoon
was full of soda and fireworks turning in some
windward direction, and you were completely unafraid.

OF CERTAIN SMALL, VALUABLE KITCHEN APPLIANCES

Take whatever it is, and call it Layer One,
and suddenly it's layers
up and around the room.

A table. People leaning over a table.

One of them is pouring maple syrup. A chrome jar
for powdered sugar.

"I've always been here," they say,
which is drawn away
or applied. Of the one and the rest.

I did not know you, and the brush of clouds
was too forceful.

I did not see where I was going
and I reached
what I can't remember what it was
I was reaching for.

Vanish the windows. Vanish this tablecloth
for this one that was always here.

That was the house with a missing wall
so we could watch. Maybe it was a table on wheels,
or there was never a table.

A counter. Some people around a table.

"Tell me a story about me," they say,
from the darkness between thoughts.

BAPTISM OF SIGNS

In the psych experiment, you're asked
to decide whether you really are
part of a psych experiment, or not.
This is clever, you think, but not as clever
as the player piano
your grandmother once owned,
or the synchronized swimming
you imagine in your sleep.

In the psych experiment, you're asked
what you dream about, when you sleep,
so you tell them
about the swimmers: how sleek
they look in their spandex costumes,
their shaved bodies. You don't tell them
about how the dogs keep barking

through every performance, or how
the courthouse roof reflects sunset's
more sinister aspirations
on evenings when the river runs low
in its dime-store camouflage.

You whistle, in the psych experiment,
which is code for telling
somebody you used to love
that yes, something has gone terribly
wrong, one of many clichés
cluttering up the food chain.
You sip your coffee
carefully, avoiding the breakwater.

In the psych experiment, sleep itself
is figured as a shy and hidden
anvil. There is the made thing
and then there is the making, the process.

You relax into Demosthenes,
that is, into myth, the damp declivities
of the old Indian graveyard.
Your progress is reflected in the Archive.
Where do the clerks go at night,
you wonder. And
what about the small churches,
their light camisoles of flannel and ash:

How do you feel about them?
How can you know what you feel?

THE WELCOME CHAMBER

In the Welcome Chamber
somebody is always waiting to help you
with your hat or your coat. Somebody is always
handing you a cold drink, if it's warm outside,
or a warm drink, if it's cold.
Somebody offers to shine your shoes.
Somebody else offers to babysit the kids
for free, if you want to go out sometime, at night.

There are beds in the Welcome Chamber,
but you never see anybody sleeping in them.
If you spill something on the furniture,
nobody minds. "We'll get it later," they say.

Each time you go to the Welcome Chamber,
you feel a little guilty. Like maybe
this is something you shouldn't be doing,
or should be doing for yourself.

You offer to help the women
with their cooking, their sewing,
their legal briefs and Gaussian equations.
"We're fine," they insist.
You make small talk
about commodity prices and the weather.
Everybody agrees with you.

You try saying "Hi." Everybody
says "Hi," back. You're so terribly afraid
somebody is about to disappoint somebody else,
and that everybody will be nice about it:

It shouldn't be so easy, you tell yourself.
There should be money involved.
There should be sirens, the almost surgical glare
of TV cameras. Somebody should be crying.
There should be dark shapes in the snow.

A FALSE SENSE OF WELL-BEING

Then there are the planets everyone can see,
delirious, but in a conservative way,
as befits our important positions in the land of slow children
and ready invitations. We passed on several courses
of the meal, practicing our ability to deny ourselves
from every third thing so that our lives stall
and catch up in a pleasantly experimental way. "Most
    anything
can work for a while," Margo said from her papier-mâché
pony, "until it starts raining or something."

So we waited for the dying to start, but it was as drawn-out
as waiting for water to boil, intent, we were sure,
on eluding nothing except us and our need at some point
to blink or otherwise self-medicate. It'll work for now
even if it's not all that clear, we decided. We'll have plenty of
    opportunities
to speak of it again, soon, when everyone's suddenly
off to far destinations
featuring delightful wineries, restaurants, and inns.

This is how we yearn these days, by saying
such things. I stand there pointing up at the sky
with my mouth open, because that's how bodies are made,
between the bank and the church, as we call out
that enough's nearly enough, isn't it. These insatiable,
    lopsided days
of sudden letters and retreats that flicker and sing to us
in blue lights and wet streets all down the coast,
with re-enactors and artisans
and how we had hoped to be a Sphinx by then.

A SHORT HISTORY OF KIKI SMITH

You walk into the gallery
and it's pink, naked, vaguely
anthropomorphic. Either it's just
one more thing to wear
on top of your head, or else
you're supposed to use it to wipe
the blood from your lips, where the flags
from the firemen's monument
have been protesting their latest
disorderly conduct citation.
You've passed some decent laws
and you're happy, most
of the time, more or less, I mean
in that way everybody keeps
talking about on the talk shows.
You could leave, of course,
but you haven't yet located
the switch for the audio component.
You think you can hear
a low, heavy gurgling
coming from somewhere
in the vicinity of Elkton, Maryland.
You think maybe this piece
is about Elkton, Maryland,
and for a few minutes you're excited,
because your great-grandmother
married her third husband
there while the rest of the country
was buried in another war.
You follow the blue velvet rope
into another room, but it's empty.
You can't decide
whether this is part of the art

or not. The truth is
Beauty does not care about us,
or not in this way. Some crows fly
over a smokestack in New Jersey
while in Los Angeles
another designer wallpaper artist
dedicates her blog to
Krishna. The little chair in the corner
is not the one you remember.
There are daughters you have,
and then there are daughters you don't.
Guess which one music's hiding.

PARABLE OF THE DOOR

You tell what's on the other side of the door
by the odor of the door.

There are rules to this game, you feel sure.
You tap the crumbling edge
of the off-season Olympic pool
impatiently, with the toe of your left foot.

All around you, fossil fuels are being liberated
from the crushing burden of use.

You want to be responsible for things
that are necessary, things nobody else does:

finishing the potato cannon. Wearing white
at unfashionable moments, like funerals.

For there to be a funeral, someone must die—
That's one rule, you're guessing. And
the politicians at the viewing, all crowded
around the little tables, with their little trays
of credit cards and baked brie with honey.

You get as close as you can to the door.
You don't smell anything, but maybe
there's a sort of humming noise
coming from the other side. You're not sure.

All the photographs in your wallet are of
politicians, honey running down their chins,

and of you, with your mouth sewn shut.

You're waiting for someone,
for the right season, only there's this terrible
pressure coming from somewhere.

Your swimsuit feels tight. It's winter.
You pretend there are orders at the factories.

I want what you've got in your hands.

NULLSTELLENSATZ

The plains around the volcano
were littered with the bodies of broken
horses, was one way of putting it.
We studied the video
of the ice-fishing championships
again and again, sixty little vice windows
coming unbraided.

The childhoods of Russian soldiers
were soft. Tourists paid
to leave their thumbprints in the matrix.

Belief, not beauty, is the basis of
autobiography, a sort of faith-healing
technique
promoted by the bourgeoisie.

In all the pharmacies, shadows
with the shape
of a governor, glancing backwards.
What a messy empire.

You cast your vote, and a corpse
adds itself to the line
in the government-subsidized cafeteria.

Kiln-fired. A postcard album
salvaged from where the two largest
rivers intersected
in the form of a panopticon,
doo-wah-diddy-dum.

It smells like bacon, but it's not. Really,
it's just something else
to wear on your head: I mean,
It's the *war* we're winning, after all.

THE LITTLE CRISIS IN SUMMER

Years go by. There's rioting
in the streets. The opposition candidate
says he's ready to be a martyr.

Maybe it's a poor translation. Years go by. The bridge
is on fire. People are jumping into the river
surrounded with parakeets. People are waving from shore.

"How can one count all the people,
when one counts so slowly," they say. A tank
moves faster. Years go by
between a window and a mirror
where you can stand on the burning bridge all night
watching yourself. People can be saved
that way. You just point, and talk in a firm, clear voice.

Say, "The ocelots are on the march." Soon enough
they'll be interested in different things, new riots
down new streets, little stands
where they sell commemorative T-shirts.

The swim team arrives. The politicians
have brought their scissors
and encouraging smiles. Soon enough, they know,
we'll reach out for each other,
just as the crowd pulls down the streetlight
and the girl in the bikini walks out and starts singing.

THE MONKEY CAGES IN WINTER

It's not as if you weren't happy.
You had your Jeep Cherokee, your stained T-shirt
reading I AM NOT YOUR EVIL EMPIRE,
and even if the snow was drifting
in from Lake Ontario, Jack-in-box, corpse-
in-copse, everything fit perfectly well

inside the ghosts you were weaving
from the stones that had fallen from the castle wall.
You checked the mile marker sign
along the suburban highway
against your body's natural temperature
set loose amid the fissured animals

nobody stops to gather, or report to the police.
This is what cell phones are for!
trumpeted the enormous billboards
erected by the pilots' union. And that was fine, too,
face cards in the spokes of some childhood
orienteering extravaganza. In this film,

you ride a jet ski toward some Caribbean paradise,
except for the long, slow tracking shot
of you methodically erasing your incorrect answers
from a tattered book of crossword puzzles.
So many things we've known
began as skills and then grew into something

more puzzling than the twisted contrails
fireworks leave against the bright patronymic
of *I'll have what she's having.*
When you sign the papers, you're reasonably sure
the dinosaurs really are extinct, although
that doesn't keep you from hoping:

that you will be the first to photograph
the funnel descending from the gravid supercell;
that the human body attracts oxygen;
that where I'm calling from
is just one more story we'll all agree on
later, a tent folded inside some color we left there.

THIS IS THE PART WHERE YOU WHISTLE

The clouds went by and so did we, just fads,
probably, we thought, in that hoping-for-ice-cream
way we'd grown so famous for
before we went hopelessly out of our minds. I remember that
from an experiment I was in once, where
I had to keep changing my pants
according to the tones from a wall speaker. I liked
several of them, where they prompt you to take
a self-guided tour. A feeling came upon me
like nausea then, some thought I'd been driving past
for years. There were children in the yards singing
"I Demand a Horizon," though I doubted they knew
what they were asking for. It was the view through a window
from a commercial for cereal that the altar boys
were so going on about, practically out of their robes
they were, and into their I LIKE BANDS T-shirts. They
named rocks and taught them tricks. They were
very good at holding their breath. I've always
wondered about that, and about myself,
as well. But what's the use in wondering,
when the schedule that the guy at the booth gave us
shows that many more things should be happening
than currently seem to be happening. I arrived.
I changed my pants a few times. I left. Why not
just say that? As there's always another model
in demand, with sale frames and years of research,
saying "I Love Goodness." The box set was still
in transit back then, though anything that rises
in a closed system could appear to be the reason
for that system. Invisible dogs on studded leashes,
for example, I-900 numbers and comment cards.

LOVE IS EVERYWHERE

The museum is full of doors that go nowhere. Each
has a train ticket
affixed to its doorknob. Some
are exterior doors, some are interior doors.

There is the sound of busy people
all around you. Kitchens maybe.

Heavy machinery. A war of some sort.

Children are there, frightened. Or maybe laughing.

And back there in the mix
is music. Mahler, maybe.

There is much you can complain about,
just as there is much for you to love.

The walls are clean
and white. The floors shine
with a real depth.

You can see yourself in reverse.

A man in a suit rolls a handful of marbles toward you,
and everything stops.

THOUSAND-YEAR REIGN

The photoshopped portraits all looked
as if someone had handed the pictures to an angel
and said, *Digitize them,* only the angel heard
Christianize them, and so instead
of something sharp we can send all over
the internet, everyone we know
now looks like an extra from a JW tract.
You said, *it was an offset job,* only I couldn't tell
if you meant "an *inside* job"
or were just making a clever pun.
In this age of digital reproduction it's easy
to wax nostalgic about the mechanism,
the clean-cut boys crouched low in toolsheds
over their conic sections. My student
places food so carefully on her Fiestaware plate
that it looks like the flag
of some small, hopeful country:
green beans left, roast beef right, mashed potatoes
down the center with a dollop of gravy
like some sort of transnational
bindi. It's the last possession, say the mediums,
but only when we pay them, which makes us
less sure about the diagnosis.
I ran into a priest at the library today, I say,
and you correct me: I ran into a man
wearing a priest's collar
at the library today. No, I didn't ask him
whether the war we wanted
was really the war the accountants deserved,
embedded in the suprachiasmatic nucleus
of language. It's dark here,
only not so dark I can't make out the night eyes
of the dead subjects in oil paintings

which follow us when we aren't looking.
When the dead rise, they will recall
every constituent atom of our livers and spleens,
and then we will explore lovely new
planets together. For now,
tiny people are boarding the ski lift,
pulling other tiny people up after them
while we watch. It's not news, but it could be
a new form of skepticism,
something we remember later, after we've
been on the news. Or rather
our photographs, looking better than we did
and speaking Italian much more fluently.

ONE HUNDRED AND ONE BEST WORLDS

Passing the fields and open skies, there's only so much
we can pretend to look for, without naming ghosts
and picturing them in lace and period costumes, punctuated
by occasional stone walls. Everything is drifting away again,
but since it started that way, and that's mostly all
we've known, there's little change beyond asking how many
levels of green there are, not proving things or asking them
really, so much as joining the tone of mile markers
checking off odd, then even, this to this,
like a girl on a bicycle on the driveway between two houses
who wants to ride, and circles work as well as
anything else. "Where I'm Calling From," they say, as one person's
trash is another's trash as well, usually, but
we may be on the verge of falling from the roof at any moment,
as any afternoon can be posed as a word problem.

It's a skill, that time you were lost in the mall
at age five. And then it becomes a shifting collage,
a narrative spun out of scraps and constructed anew
with every mall you visit. I couldn't remember
what happened, of course. It's an essential part
of forgetting, which is what we spend most of our time
doing. There was a field, that much is certain. Was it you
or me, who got dragged there? And in what way
might it be testable? Because the story is almost
the same thing as any other story you make up,
except that the more you tell it, the more unstable
it becomes. One of us is driving. There are fields. And
occasionally, we'll turn to each other and say "field,"
and the other will agree, and then suddenly to the side
is the field, that one, as some improvised solution
that works. The surprise of that. The giftlike quality.

HAVING A SENSE OF PURPOSE

It's not about that person over there near the exit,
the one who looks like he wants to slip out,
but let's pretend it is for now, so that
we can be kind of clueless about what's going on
and it can be kind of fun, with your diamond cigarette
and the illusion of Elvis that weaves its way
through the potted plants and sudden calls
from down the line for calm and reasonableness. We have time
to be many things and none of them for long,
so we can certainly understand the liminal motivation
of a red EXIT sign illuminating so much more than
a one-inch border and a sudden feeling
for lost connections. There's a haze rising
over the begonias, reminding us of the famous battle
of Lake Erie in 1813, where the boats turned into swans
and erected a little thatch hut they named The Blue Zone,
where, when you stay, you are encouraged to shower
with your shoes on. O. H. Perry would later
tell us that what looks to be one thing is in fact
many things, and each of them a little turtle
that one can raise as one's own. But memory changes
over time, and that woman at the door was more
sinned against than sinning, as we all meant
to pay attention, but the future kept getting
in the way. "Remember those begonias," Margo asks,
"how they told us to press a key whenever we were aware
we were no longer paying attention? How
those begonias kept me up nights, such as
reflecting on personal experiences or picturing yourself
at a little Inn at Put-in-Bay, where we were maybe more able
to think most deeply about the big picture,
navigating between near-term and long-term
planting instructions. We weren't as nice to the little creature

as we could have been, and for that we're sorry,
but even so, it was we who had to stay there and pick up
after them, and find out that sometimes there is no
last laugh, unless it's the sound of something like water
in the other room, spilling across a table."

THE SAHARA AS ANECDOTE

It's the perfect and fitting afternoon
for both of us, driving across the dunes of East Timor,
not caring if East Timor has dunes or not,
and yes, it was just like any other fireworks display,
except we had to watch them at the conceptual level,
and some of the components
that are not supposed to react with each other
do anyway. "How is one supposed to know such things
in the middle of the explosion," we asked,
as the map replaced the territory,
and certain reactions don't happen
that should. I thought of everything I could
for several seconds. The falling
buildings. Which sock goes on first. Which
shoe. The people running. The mall. The way we stood there
on a little rise watching the moon and the sun
pass each other. From where we stood,
the sun is 400 times larger than the moon,
and it's 400 times farther away,
so that they appear the same size, with a little diamond
attached. People grew fearful and asked others
to marry them, proof that everything that can happen
does, and with a little freckle
of doubt. "I'm going to be a good girl now,"
I believe we said. And once you put these bricks together
you can go. And once you do something
with these dogs. Look at how small
the buildings are, and how lax the security. I prayed
for air conditioning. I felt sorry for those people.

PARABLE OF THE ANORAK IN THE RAIN

The smell of a hand. The sound of some faces
and we were that slightly open
door or window, I mean, it seemed
light was somebody else's daughter looking
through us, the way food does
on the television or the radio. We're built

to take it like that, pre-stressed.
And surrounded by so great a cloud of
microwaves, which is why the autistic children
flap their hands in air.
They see it, they're waving at it,
they want it to notice them. They want air

to bring them a present, or speak a soft syllable
in the language they understand,
which is numbers. The machines rage
against the politicians, yes, but
in time; it only takes a few elided votes

to make your BlackBerry nonfunctional
the minute the train enters the darkened tunnel
where gender's being held hostage
by our memories of bees.
Understand: there are no guesses,

only fewer birds in the park, and fewer
cell phone ring tones
for them to emulate in the ecstasy of sex.
The threshold you apprehend

is merely a latent nausea brought on
by your grandmother's emigration. There is a

loneliness buried deep inside
Canada, inside all the blurry videos of Canada
waiting for the masked seraphim to speak

in golden plates. Here's how you put on
clothing, when you're cold, and here's
how you take it off again, when you're done.
I'm sorry, Mr. President.
I can't touch what's burned into my tongue.

IN PRAISE OF HARD CANDY

There is a danger in fashion and it means
what the mannequins do
when the credit industry slips
out of alignment, which is basically
nothing, only nobody's really sure about that.

You take an ax from the bracketed wall
only to see it's a fire ax, meaning
it's there for the purpose of saving something
while destroying something else,

relying on body heat
to illuminate the invisible handwriting
on the slave trader's bill of sale.
I want to say I'm carrying a live honeybee
in my mouth, but I'm not;

I envy the aircraft
pretty much everything except for
its anhydrous stigmata, its ammoniac gills.
Ghost, we say, and when we say it,
we mean *Ghost.* The radio left on
inside City Hall after hours.
The police desk blotter. Surveillance
is not a form of torture
we recognize when we pass it in the street

but more delicate, *I can't hear you*
vs. *The water is running,* something electricity
wrote in its childhood diary,
Beauty's been watching me again vs. *Don't leave
your umbrella on board this black train.*

THIS IS A WOLF WITH MANY SHARP TEETH

At the St. Laszlo Motor Inn and Food Court,
it's back to the pudding, to discuss the leaves across
the parking lot, and the waning days
of the burn ban, watching our fingernails grow.

"Isn't that nice," we say, looking up from the game
at some truth mud-wrestling with a watermelon,
that we catch and then lose, and wonder immediately
what we might know about a truth's ability
to stand up to such things, and if maybe someone's
supposed to eat the watermelon later. By later,
we mean Tom Sawyer in a cave
with Becky Thatcher, playing something soft
on the ukulele. With that, we hopped right off the end
of the hopscotch board, into the vodka marigolds.

"Long time no see," we murmured to each other
as we fell upon the tables, throwing caution
to the workers who appeared in dire need. It wasn't
that large-spirited of us, so don't get your gum
in a wad or anything. It was a Saturday. Ladies
were drinking free. The boys were playing in the yard,
putting sand in their shoes, calling it "an analogy."

Midnight was coming late that month. We only had time
for a few more minutes, until they changed the filter
and had to fire the boom operator,
as we realized we were older by then, and had already
said our good-byes, but there was still quite a bit of politeness
to fill. Well. I guess this is what pinochle
is for. Can we get it to last twenty years? Here,
help me with the ladder. This traffic is insufferable.
It's all one juggle, one vanishing.

SINGLE-CELLED ORGANISM

We've left the waders in the pond, and
all the supernumerary planets. It's getting hot in here,
someone says, and the voice
is almost like
an artifact you recollect, vaguely,
from your grandmother's pinchbeck jewelry box.

It feels as if many people are watching
television while you read this.

New England isn't all it's cracked up to be,
is one problem. And getting lost
amid exterior definitions
is another, all flaking paint and outsized lachrymosa.
I'm not exactly sure who let the newspapers

die—were we in the vineyards?
Was everything perfect, and did we remember
to e-mail that to the editor?
We used to sit out on the lawn,
or rather, on old quilts spread out on the lawn, and

there was this beautiful music
coming from somewhere. Now people form lines
waiting for the next part,
which is us, too, but with better lighting.
BASED ON A TRUE STORY, the buildings say,

which is kind of them, really,
to think of us, now that we travel exclusively
by glass, so that we can see
one another, and where we're going,

the humidity chanting the same old incantations,
Soffit, football, deer park, cousin,
complete strangers executing perfect dance moves
in the cupped hollow of your rotary phone.

PRAISE IMPROMPTU

It's one of those trick pictures of yourself
where you're multiplied, sitting in a circle
of yourselves, interspersed with mannequins
attempting to define the color blue. The idea
of blue, as there's always more than you can see,
there on a lawn full of dead birds
that we call dead bird lawn for the rest of the summer.

It's how we attempt modesty, as we've ended
so many things in so many ways
everything begins to look like ice cream
and raspberries. Here's some applesauce, for instance,
or here, come lean against me. Wave
to your old lovers. All the bell towers of America
are starting up "My Favorite Things"
in unison, followed by something I don't recognize.

The rat in the car in the dog
in the boar, or however the song goes, the song goes
into the song, and you don't catch the title,
so now you have to go around saying, "You know, the one
that goes, 'Oooo baby,' or something," as babies
are falling from the sky.

You still have all the same kind of interesting thoughts
you've always had, it's just that now
you can't seem to do anything with them. You look
out the window and all the houses are
open. Doors, windows,
all open. They opened the flues. They've run
into the yards with baskets and exact change.

ON THE FALL OF CONSTANTINOPLE

Critique is destiny. At the wedding reception,
you find your way into the museum
of unguarded intentions and then
back out again, only this time you're wearing
some different clothing and you're no longer sure

what it means to "be a good person."
Synanon became just one more way
of mourning the inevitable, *viz.*
how highway always gives way to more highway.
Your daughter comes home from college

and wants to know just what lichens *are*
and what was Stanley Kubrick
trying to get at with that blue
food business. Ribbons of ocean
are running inside the container corporations

faster than the shrimp fleets can keep up.
Is this how Chinese ideograms happen
when we aren't watching? You broil a TV
dinner inside the Capitol
and start paging through the manual.

It's so hard to guess what's going to happen
when gun control and birth control
get switched at the laundry.
You run through the woods, and then you film
yourself running through the woods:

Nobody knows which direction
the entertainment is really coming from.
Nobody knows who's chasing you,

or the little song the green leaves are singing
as they honeymoon in the rain.

EXTERNAL SONATA

It's always someone else's story that has the accident.
Some story tired of traveling
and highly distractible. The other stories know this.
They hear it in the popular songs.

We stop paying attention to it, but luckily for us,
so does everyone else.
No one has to feel left out.

The story changes its name,
moves next door, and starts working on the lawn,
humming little tunes.
I go back and forth to the mailbox. I've been trying
to make out this signature all afternoon.

If any of us were blameless,
I wouldn't know it. Not written this way,
or if there's the possibility that it's an important story
whose realized projects fare about as well
as the unrealized ones.

I make a prediction every spring. Every spring,
there's this accident.

Still, I felt they were daring us
to think it funny, so we thought it funny,
even if we didn't know what we were laughing at
or if it was what they thought we were laughing at,
tears streaming down our faces,
imagining other lawn chairs, other barbecues.

PORTRAIT WHILE YOU WAIT

"Thank you, it's been good," we say, and the next story
is coming up soon. And so we set the clocks
back to 10:10 again, and we're sure
we're going to collapse
from the tension. Seems like the same lesson
applies to us all, over and over. Take Socrates, for instance,
or fishing, and then you're older than that
the rest of your life.

At the return engagement, there's always
a moral equivalence between "I'm just a simple potter"
and "My associations with them
are purely ceremonial." Either way,
you have to get the house in shape. And, knock wood,
I have never gotten so far.

Still, all the smoke, you know? You don't just
wander around dreaming. That's not
what you get paid for, after the Bichons Frisés,
the migraines, the sentimentality cloaked
in sappiness. Now, you just tell me everything
you've been up to, as I keep getting the two of us confused,
we look so alike, and with so little to show for it,
as each outfit comes up solely from the outfit just before it
and stays only as far as the next restaurant.

I had a lot to say to you, several meanings worth,
at least. "I saw you in the park," was one. "If you know
what I mean," was another, but none of the doors
in that house would close properly, the divining rod
didn't fit, and your cousin died suddenly. All these expected
      things
that continually surprise us, as we're getting to the drive-in late

just as the gnats begin circling, with so many questions
not to ask, so many answers not to have.

ON LIBERALISM

You're supposed to be watching a documentary
about the riots. Somehow, you've been left
here, in this cold classroom, alone, with a video monitor.
People you don't know keep walking into
and out of the room, but nobody else stays.

You turn on the monitor. You see
the image of a small girl, dressed up, as if
for a party. She's walking away from the camera
through what might be a fallow field,
or maybe a vacant city lot. The frame of the image
doesn't allow for much, in terms of context.

This seems to go on for a long time.
The figure of the girl recedes into some vague distance.
You wonder what this has to do with the riots.

When the image of the girl has finally disappeared
into indistinguishable pixels, she's replaced
by a series of talking heads: a politician,
a clergyman in vestments,
what looks like an African American
college professor, then a young white man in jeans
cradling a lamb in his arms.
They all seem to be speaking passionately
about something, only there's no sound.

After a while the talking heads give way
to scenes from a construction site: lots of reinforced
concrete and steel, heavy cranes, ant-sized men
shouting things you can't quite make out
because even though the sound now seems to be back on,
the voices are drowned out by the machinery.

It's getting late. You're still wondering
what this all has to do with the riots, what it was
you were supposed to be learning, why there's oil
on your shirt, your burnt face, and your hands.

THE DREAM OF EGYPT

In the dream, we're floating
down a long corridor
lined with flowered wreaths,

the sort you see at funerals.

We're not exactly happy
about this, but we're not exactly
unhappy, either.
It's that sort of dream.

In the dream, or what
we remember of the dream,
we are thinking
ahead, mostly, towards
what is coming,
what we are approaching.

It isn't clear that this
has anything to do with us,
really, only that we are on our
way somewhere.

Some of the flowers
smell good. Some of them
seem to be made of wax,
or plastic.

Sometimes we think
we hear music, floating back
to us from somewhere
farther down the corridor,
ahead, in the distance.

A guitar maybe, or a trumpet.

There are worse things
than music, you tell me,
reaching for the knife
I find I'm holding in my hand.

Here, let me show you.

PAIN CAN WARN US OF DANGER

And pain is bureaucratic, where we find ourselves
along the Stockholm Archipelago, saying
thanks for taking care of me, and thanks
for giving me food. And then some other name for it
like elections, or waiting for elections. We called,
but it just went to your voicemail. We were
worried, as you were talking about money,
and we said you'll have money again, sometime
later, but we weren't sure, really, and perhaps you heard it
in our tone . . . so there's a concept, and then
a town to fill it. Everyone gets hurt or dies
and then is better right away. Things dodder
along, and sometimes memorably. We like that. And
why not want that again? You know what happens
when one tries to replicate the past—yes, but
what if one tries to replicate something that
didn't work out all that well? That maybe this
completes it—like that time we pretended downtown
Denver was in Paris, and we could break up
over some wine and mixed blessings. And in this story
there are no characters, which is first a word
and then people thinking, calling it The Dubious
Age. There are no dogs out there barking,
you realize. And then you think, I'm going
to be reasonable for the rest of the afternoon. I'm going
to cover my cough and clean my hands for more
than twenty seconds. When we were happiest,
we did such things. And we'll be happy again, against
the backdrop of the mountains, ordering wine.

ON THE DEATH OF ANDREW WYETH

There's a green place, you think,
and a river, from just inside the airliner
where the restaurant has just
touched down. The captain is taking
a bow, the passengers are taking a bow,
waiters in evening wear lead them all
past the commemorative buffet.

The dancers are knocking
at the locked doors of the abandoned
warehouse. They shiver in the cold.
Nobody answers, nobody lets them in.

The restaurant moves slowly,
either with or against the current.
The president appears as a holograph
on the backside of a dollar bill.

In the green place, you think,
scientists will deliver the evidence
to the people who need it most,
in holiday packaging: the DNA
samples, the pharmaceutical trials,
confetti from the postal strike.

From the basements of courthouses,
their dingy walk-ups and coldwater flats,
the dancers will unpeel each piece
of evidence from every other
piece of evidence, examining closely
what it was we said we wanted,

or thought we wanted. They will speak
calmly to the lawyers and TV
cameras. They will move gracefully
out of the doorways the survivors
keep making, they will keep bringing us
our beautiful, irrefutable names.

WELCOME TO THE NEXT PROJECT

Over the side of each new action
is taped a note informing us of its meaning. We're certain of it,
and so we keep the notes in neat piles,
hoping next week or so to find someone
who can read that language
and save us from the extravagant nature of our guessing.

It got us through the city though, past the evidentiary
and revolution,
past the museum displays of the kitchens
of the future, lemony fresh. The signs all said
Happy People Frighten Us and
Are You a Good Witch or a Bad Witch? You said this one thing
to your father and then fathers were done, and you
had to pick up his clothes
and do something with them. And what of the ones
that were nice? That you wouldn't mind wearing? It's easy.
Just call it a project. Count the museums by twos.
Already it starts to feel uncomfortably similar
to the last project, like any day of the year
with typical weather.

You begin to feel so defeated.

I'll board up the house. Take down the book.
It's getting near the last page, we're going
to have to turn back or give up soon.

It was a good year for the roses, even so, as outside
of each new action is taped another action. We left the city
to visit your mother, your father. They look at you
the way children do, because you can't help them,
and you kept telling them you always would.

AFTER MUSIC

In the moment after music
we are instructed not to remember
the sounds the children made
as the bombs kept falling, and then,
after, the dripping of rainwater
from the copper eaves, the boughs
of splintered plane trees.

Instead, recall the way the bridges
at dusk seemed to join
mathematics with some other
country, all the people out walking
backwards and forwards like tourists,
Touch not, taste not, handle not.

After music, we look into the mirror
and see thieves dispossessing
the republic of its treasures, then
taking trolleys out to where
the suburbs are about to begin.
Relax, murmur the pharmacologists
from their black-box cafés,
the policemen from their kiosks.

There is this enormous silence
inside music, where the people
in photographs go when we
are no longer there to watch them,
where the dreams of small houses
keep awaiting new shoes.

A bridge requires a body, a human
form sealed inside like an IOU

or a letter from a lover you will never
open. The bombs stop falling, and then
all the people come out walking:

Look, they say, *This was a river,*
this was a school. The sunlight chants,
There is no suburb, there is no other side.

ACKNOWLEDGMENTS

The authors deeply appreciate the succor and indulgence of the editors of the following journals, in which many of these poems appeared, some in earlier versions:

32 Poems: "Different from What You Bargained For"
Alaska Quarterly Review: "The Carnegie System"
Anti-: "The Other Palace, "External Sonata," "Love Is Everywhere," "On Your Smooth Ride"
Antioch Review: "The Welcome Chamber" (also appeared on the *Poetry Daily* website)
Booth: "The City Experiment," "Meditation on Subjects"
Boston Review: "From This Mortar Cities Rise"
BRAND: "The Baby Catalogues," "Elegy for Rosa Parks"
Cannibal: "Thousand-Year Reign"
CANT: "If I Die Before I Wake," "How Are Things in Glocca Morra," "Can't You Sit Still for Once"
Christianity & Literature: "After the War, the Orchards"
Coconut: "In the File of Discontinued Things"
Colorado Review: "Error as Beauty," "Automated Town"
Connotation Press: "Daily Life in Classical Antiquity"
Copper Nickel: "Landscape with Missing Elements," "All Trains Leaving Penn Station Are Ghost Trains"
Court Green: "In Praise of Hard Candy"
Crazyhorse: "The House Rhapsody," "Anniversaries of Bad Things," "The Dream of Egypt," "Everything You Know That Isn't True"
Cutbank: "Nullstellensatz," "The Monkey Cages in Winter"
Del Sol Review: "The History of Entanglements"
Denver Quarterly: "Elemental Picture of Boats in the Distance," "Space to the West"
Diode: "Your Father on the Train of Ghosts," "On the Death of Andrew Wyeth," "Pharaoh's Daughter (Chagall Motion Study)"
Ecotone: "On a Raft, Relaxing into the West, Where We Are"
FIELD: "The Bridge at Rest"

Fifth Wednesday: "Your Father Seen from Space," "Your Father Calling from the Museum"

Forklift, Ohio: "Aromatherapy in the Age of New Form," "On the Fall of Constantinople"

Front Porch: "Your New Birthday," "Advice to Passengers"

Gulf Coast: "Busman's Holiday," "On the Solitary Death of the Woolworth Building"

Handsome: "The Anodynes"

Harp & Altar: "On Liberalism"

Harvard Review: "Parable of the Anorak in the Rain"

Interim: "The World Is Empty & a Splash of Salts," "Praise Impromptu," "The Little Crisis in Summer"

Jet Fuel Review: "Limited Time Offer," "Box with Noise Elements," "Ethel & Myrtle Try To Avoid How Emotional They Get," "Your Hands as the Third Law of Motion," "Of Certain Small, Valuable Kitchen Appliances," "This Is the Part Where You Whistle"

The Journal: "The Archaeologists," "University Park," "A False Sense of Well-Being," "Maybe It Has Nothing To Do with You"

Jubilat: "The Sherpas of Canada"

Kenyon Review: "Pain Can Warn Us of Danger," "The Tourist," (online) "Your Reply Is Necessary"

Lo-Ball: "I'll Decorate My House with You"

Memorious: "The Overgrown War"

MiPoesias: "Elegy for the Most People," "Gun Control in the Occupation," "The Circus of Probable Sighs," "The Great Migrations"

The Nation: "Trade Deficit"

New England Review: "Your Lover, Later"

New Orleans Review: "Making Love in the Balloon Maze," "Candling the Bodies"

Ninth Letter: "My Father in Other Places"

Notre Dame Review: "On the Performativity of Grief as Ecstatic Gesture," "Elegy for the Manhattan Project"

Pleiades: "Elegy for Henrietta Lacks," "Outside the Elevator Museum," "Halls of Fame II"

Poetry International: "Another Day at the Festival," "After Music," "Ideal Boating Conditions," "And as They Waited on the Hillsides, It Began To Rain"

Poetry London: "Baptism of Signs"

Poetry Northwest: "A Short History of Friendship," "Cedar Rapids Eclogue," "Trenton Aubade"

A Public Space: "Scandinavian Skies"

Quarterly West: "Domestic Light"

Raleigh Quarterly: "Welcome to the Next Project," "Elegy for the Developing Story"

Saltgrass: "Single-Celled Organism," "The Night Autopsy," "You Need Not Be Present To Win"

Southern Review: "The Radio inside Your Health Plan Is Sleeping," "As Mastery Declines into Altitude & Forgiveness"

Tight: "In the Later Measures," "Winter Acknowledgments"

TYPO: "Parable of the Door"

Washington Square: "Ode to Lyndon Baines Johnson," "A Short History of Kiki Smith"

Western Humanities Review: "Because It's Better Not To Know," "The Birthday Hand"

"The Solitary Death of the Woolworth Building" takes its title from a work by Louise Bourgeois. The title "Stolen Crutch, Wrapped in Yarn" refers to an artwork by Judith Scott.

"The Sherpas of Canada" is for Thom Ward. "Apology Re: The Second Viennese School" is for David Shohl. "Cesarean Selection" was for Jennifer Mackenzie, and "On a Raft, Relaxing into the West, Where We Are" for John Lane. "Another Day at the Festival" is in memory of Craig Arnold.

Special thanks to Kevin Prufer, Tony Farrington, Ilya Kaminsky, and John Cross for reading earlier versions of this manuscript.

ABOUT THE AUTHORS

G.C. Waldrep's previous collections of poetry include *Goldbeater's Skin* (2003), winner of the Colorado Prize; *Disclamor* (BOA, 2007); and *Archicembalo* (2009), winner of the Dorset Prize. His work has appeared in many journals, including *Poetry, Ploughshares, APR, Boston Review, New England Review, Threepenny Review, Colorado Review, Tin House, Harper's,* and *The Nation*, as well as in *The Best American Poetry 2010*. He was a 2007 National Endowment for the Arts Fellow in Literature and received a 2008 Gertrude Stein Award for Innovative American Poetry. His anthology of creative, critical, and personal responses to the life and work of Paul Celan, co-edited with Ilya Kaminsky, is forthcoming from Marick Press. He lives in Lewisburg, Pennsylvania, where he teaches at Bucknell University, directs the Bucknell Seminar for Younger Poets, and serves as Editor-at-Large for *The Kenyon Review*.

John Gallaher's previous collections of poetry include *The Little Book of Guesses* (2007), winner of the Levis poetry prize, and *Map of the Folded World* (2009). His work has appeared in such journals as *Field, Denver Quarterly, Ploughshares, New American Writing, Colorado Review,* and *The Kenyon Review*, as well as in *The Best American Poetry 2008*. In 2010, he won the *Boston Review* poetry prize. He is currently co-editor of *The Laurel Review*, and, with Mary Biddinger, The Akron Series in Contemporary Poetics.

BOA EDITIONS, LTD.
AMERICAN POETS CONTINUUM SERIES

COLOPHON

Your Father on the Train of Ghosts, poems by G.C. Waldrep and John Gallaher, is set in Centaur, a digitalized version of the font designed for Monotype by Bruce Rogers in 1928. The italic, based on drawings by Frederic Warde, is an interpretation of the work of the sixteenth-century printer and calligrapher Ludovico degli Arrighi, after whom it is named.

The publication of this book is made possible, in part, by the special support of the following individuals:

Anonymous
Joseph Belluck, *in honor of* Bernadette Catalana
Pete & Bev French
Anne Germanacos
Janice N. Harrington & Robert Dale Parker
Christopher Kennedy & Mi Ditmar
X. J. Kennedy
Rosemary & Lew Lloyd
Boo Poulin
Deborah Ronnen & Sherman Levey
Steven O. Russell & Phyllis Rifkin-Russell
Vicki & Richard Schwartz
Ellen & David Wallack
Glenn & Helen William